# Restored

## ELEVEN GIFTS FOR A COMPLETE LIFE

Tracy J. Trost

DESTINY IMAGE® PUBLISHERS, INC.

P.O. Box 310, Shippensburg, PA 17257-0310

*"Speaking to the Purposes of God for This Generation and for the Generations to Come."*

This book and all other Destiny Image, Revival Press, MercyPlace, Fresh Bread, Destiny Image Fiction, and Treasure House books are available at Christian bookstores and distributors worldwide.

For a U.S. bookstore nearest you, call 1-800-722-6774.

For more information on foreign distributors, call 717-532-3040.

Reach us on the Internet: www.destinyimage.com.

ISBN 13 TP: 978-0-7684-3516-0
ISBN 13 HC: 978-0-7684-3517-7
ISBN 13 LP: 978-0-7684-3518-4
ISBN 13 Ebook: 978-0-7684-9057-2

For Worldwide Distribution, Printed in the U.S.A.

1 2 3 4 5 6 7 8 / 14 13 12 11 10

*Spoiler Alert*

*D*ear Reader

This book is a collection of letters from a man (Sam) to his daughter. The character of Sam, though he is fictional, is passing down life lessons to his daughter that are very much real. It is very important that before you read this book you have either watched the movie *A Christmas Snow* or read the novel *A Christmas Snow* written by Jim Stovall, author of *The Ultimate Gift*. This will allow you to understand who Sam is and why he is writing these letters. Plus if you watch the movie or read the book after reading *Restored* it will spoil the surprise ending for you. Thank you for reading this book, I hope it will open your life to new and greater things.

TRACY J. TROST

# Contents

# Foreword

## By Jim Stovall

You are preparing to embark on a life-altering journey within the pages of this book you hold in your hands. Your tour guide for this journey is my friend and colleague Tracy Trost. Tracy will not be leading you on Sam's journey only. He will be leading you on a journey of your own as well.

There are some books that entertain, there are others that educate, and there are a few very special books that transform. If you will allow it to, this book will transform your life.

One of my partners in the movie *The Ultimate Gift*, based on one of my novels, was fond of saying, "If you can tell a great story, you earn the right to share a message." Through Tracy Trost's screenplay and the subsequent movie entitled *A Christmas Snow*, along with the novel I was privileged to write with the same title, we introduced some characters who have taken on a life of their own and are affecting people around the world. This book will give you a deeper look into the lives and spirits of those people you met in *A Christmas Snow*.

I hope as you follow Sam's story, you will consider your own life and your own destiny.

I have the privilege of speaking to countless people around the world in arena events as well as through my books, columns, and movies. I believe the most important message I can share is that the life we are living right now is not a practice game. This is the World Series, the Super Bowl, and the Olympics all rolled up into one. If you do not feel that kind of power and passion about what you do all day every day, you need to find something new to do or find a new attitude immediately.

Changing your life is a simple matter of changing your mind. You will notice that I did not say it was easy. I only said it was simple. Many people know this, but few actually do it. In today's society, when it's all said and done, there's a lot more said than actually done. People spend more time planning their three-day weekend than they spend planning the rest of their life. You have the freedom and the opportunity to contemplate your future and, through word and deed, bring it into reality.

Tracy and I are serious about providing quality entertainment and a great value for your investment of time and money into books and movies; however, I have long believed I am not in the book, movie, column, speech, or television business. I am in the message business. That message is designed to help you create the life for yourself and for those around you that you were intended to live.

I hope you will take the challenge within these pages and then share it with others in your world.

JIM STOVALL

Author, *A Christmas Snow*

# A Note From the Author

The book you are about to read is the story of one man's journey through life. Sam could be you or me. He is just an average man. Much like most people, he has and has had hopes, dreams, and desires. Through the decisions he has made, he unknowingly charted a course for his life. If you could talk with him today, I am sure he would tell you that there are things he wishes he could do over. He would probably tell you that the worst day of his life was the day he walked out the door, leaving behind his family and—most of all—his little girl.

I am sure there are events in your life that you wish you could do over. I know there are in mine. In fact, I am sure every person walking on this Earth wishes he or she had a couple "do-overs." It's vital to remember that it's not what happens to us in life that is important; it's what we do with it that matters. We all have things happen to us that we don't have control over, but the one thing that we do have control over is how we respond. This is where the choices and decisions come in.

Our lives are what they are based on the choices and decisions we have made. We will be who we are going to be starting with the choices and decisions we make today. Life is full of experiences—good things and bad things happen to each and every one of us. The way we react and handle these things defines us as individuals.

Do you let the events of the past dictate who you are and what you can and cannot do now or in the future? Or do you decide who you are and what your future is going to be? The choices are yours to make—every moment of every day of your life.

S. Albert Mitchell, or Sam, as his friends know him, made some bad decisions during his life journey, and he used them to build a foundation for his life. He allowed the bad choices his father made to form his belief system. Even though he hated that belief system, he replicated it in his life. Until we make a conscious decision to think differently, we will think as we have been trained. Sam did that very thing, and the choices and decisions he made became his life.

But one day he was introduced to the Truth. This Truth opened his mind and allowed him to see there was another way of thinking. This Truth showed him that he had the ability to determine who and what he will be merely by changing the way he thought of himself. Sam came to a life-transforming knowledge of his Creator. Because one man shared the truths of the teaching of Christ, he was able to transform his life. He was able to apply these truths and see life in a whole new dimension.

Please don't be fooled and think it was all easy after that. In some ways, his life became harder. He still had a lifetime of bad decisions and habits to overcome, but now he had hope—in the past, he had none.

In this journal, you will find a collection of letters that Sam wrote to his daughter while on his way to find her 25-plus years after he had left her and his wife. Sam's desire is to give his daughter the most valuable gift of all—Truth.

Like Sam, I have learned that the most valuable things in life cannot be held in your hands. They are the life-transforming truths that God has given us—including the power to follow His destiny for us and fulfill our dreams.

It is my desire that the truths brought to you from Sam's experiences will help you let go of past hurts and give you a vision and hope for your victorious future.

My good friend Jim Stovall once made a statement during one of our very valuable talks. He said, "Every man can see, but not every man has vision. Sight shows you where you are today. Vision shows you where you will be tomorrow." Use the truths of Sam's journal to help you gain a vision for your future.

To your success,

TRACY J. TROST

# December 24, Faith

## Seattle, Washington

My Dearest Kathleen,

I don't really know how to start this letter. The last time I saw you was Christmas Eve over 25 years ago. I know you must hate me and not want to hear from me, but I need to let you know that it wasn't your fault that I left. You may not believe this, but leaving that night was the hardest thing I have ever done in my life. I believed that if I stayed, I would continue to do you and your mother harm.

I am writing to you today because something extraordinary has happened to me over the past year. Since you last saw me, I have traveled all over the United States. I tried to make a name for myself in business, but one job after another ended in failure because of my destructive lifestyle. Every time I failed, I blamed those around me, and I would drink away my pain.

Over the years I took part-time jobs, and I was always on the move. I guess I thought there would be a better opportunity in the next town, but the truth was I was just running. Running from myself I guess, and running from you.

Please know that there was not a day that went by that I didn't think of you. You were always in my thoughts and many times my reason to keep going and try again. I guess I thought that if I could have even a little bit of success, that I could show you and make you proud of me.

I have been on a bus a dozen times making my way back to see you. But I always abandoned the plan when I got close. The thought of seeing you is filled with joy and great pain.

For the past couple of years I have been in the Seattle area. I had a job here and I thought that I was going to be able to save some money and make contact with you. Then the market dropped, and once again I was out of a job. I looked for months for a new job but ended up on the streets again.

This may sound strange, but the street was comforting to me. I wouldn't wish that life-style on anyone, but for me it became a comfort zone in my life. No one expects anything from you there. You don't have to prove yourself to anyone. I lived in that mind-set for the past 25 years. But now everything is different. I don't know how to explain it, but even the street is different to me now.

I was staying at a local mission downtown when I was asked to attend a church service. A young man named Jason was sharing from the Bible that night. He was telling the story of Jesus' birth—the same story I've heard my whole life. You know the story, born from a virgin in a manger. We have all heard it. But then he told another story—the story of Simeon, an old priest who was in the temple when Jesus, as a baby, was brought to be dedicated to the Lord.

This story interested me because I had never heard it before. Simeon was an old man who was a priest in the temple. When he was a younger man, he had a vision from God. He was told that he would not die before seeing the Christ, the salvation of the world. He held on to that dream his whole life.

When Jesus was born, it was a custom for the Jewish people to take their children to the temple to be blessed. Joseph and Mary took Jesus to the temple on the eighth day of his life. When they arrived at the temple, they were greeted by Simeon, who took the baby in his arms. When he looked into the baby's eyes, he began to weep. He held the baby up and he blessed him. Then he said something that took Joseph and Mary by surprise. He looked toward the sky and said, "Sovereign Lord, as You have promised, You may now dismiss your servant in peace. For my eyes have seen Your salvation, which You have prepared in the sight of all people, a light for revelation to the Gentiles and for glory to Your people Israel."

It is believed that he died very soon after the encounter.

Kathleen, I feel very much like Simeon in that it was at the end of my life that I saw God's Salvation. After a lifetime of bad choices and decisions, I finally found what I had been searching for my entire life. I always felt as though I had a hole in my life. I tried to fill it with all sorts of things—women, booze, material possessions, money, and anything else I thought would bring happiness.

After the service at the mission, for some reason I stayed until everyone else had left. I just sat there thinking of the story and my life. Then Jason came to me and asked if he could talk with me. I'm not sure why I said yes, but I felt the young man had something that I had been looking for—something to fill the empty hole.

He asked to hear my story, and for some reason I told him. I told him about how I left you when you were just ten years old. I told him how looking back at you through the window on that cold Christmas Eve is still etched in my memory. I told him how the memories of you as a child have never left me—they actually haunt me and remind me every day of my poor excuse for a life. I opened up about my other failed marriages. I am sure you don't know this, but I have been married to two other women besides your mother. Both ended the same way, me running away.

It was strange. I didn't know this man, but I felt safe telling him my story. I felt that I could tell him anything, and he wouldn't judge me. He sat there for hours listening as I dumped my pathetic life on his lap.

When I was finally finished, I was broken. I let go of a lifetime of pain. I was embarrassed, and again I wanted to run. He just looked at me and smiled. He told me that my life could change if I wanted. He told me that there was a source of unlimited forgiveness available to every person. He said all I had to do was be willing to see life differently. See it and then believe it. I told him that I was not a religious person. He said he wasn't, either. He said religion had nothing to do with it. It is belief, a belief so strong that my life will change as a result.

That night was the beginning of my life-changing experience. There was no choir singing or bright light shining down on me, but for the first time in my life I started to see things differently—to realize that the Creator of my life did not hate me because of my bad decisions. To think that He was actually interested in my life gave me...well it gave me hope! For the first time in as long as I can remember, I felt hope. I have to tell you, it was like drinking an ice-cold glass of water on a hot day. Refreshing and full of life.

For the first time, I felt as though the huge weight that I had been carrying around could be lifted. I was able to believe that my life didn't have to be this way. Believe me, I don't know how it works, all I know is it does. When Jason told me of this salvation and relationship with my Creator, all I did was be willing to believe it. From that point on, everything was different. I wish I could explain it better to you, but I have no words that can describe it other than life changing.

I started meeting with Jason and his family on a regular basis. I spent a lot of time with him and his family. It was an incredible experience, but when I was alone at night, all I could think of was you and all the pain I had caused you.

Kathleen, there is never a day that I don't think of you and of that night I walked out of your life. I hope that one day we can meet again and that I can be part of your life. I have a lifetime of regrets that I am working through, but it is my hope that one day we can be together again.

I am going to keep this journal to share my life with you until we meet face to face. I have learned in this long life of mine that things of real value are not things you can hold in your hands. Things of real value have eternal impact. They are the Life Lessons passed on from a father to his daughter. I know that I was not there as your father throughout your life, but I hope that you would consider these lessons for your life and pass them on to your children.

The first life gift that I give to you is the *Gift of Faith*.

I lived my life without any type of faith or hope for any kind of outcome other than to satisfy my own personal wants, needs, and desires. I was so self-centered that I was able to leave you and your mother for what I thought was best for me and my life.

I had no faith in God or any higher power. I was empty, and I made decisions based on trying to fill that eternal hole with temporary items. It never worked.

It was not until I was willing to open my heart to God and realize that by His grace and His mercy that I can have a life of hope.

Katy, I have found what I have been searching for my whole life. It is faith. Faith that my life has a purpose, faith that one day I will see you again, faith that God cares for me, and faith that I am loved.

This gift has made my life worth living. It has given me a reason to go on. So my first life gift to you is the gift of faith.

# February 28, Courage

## Seattle, Washington

I was able to get a job at the Street Mission where I have been staying. I help out with the janitorial work and pick up after the men. Today I was helping serve dinner. I was clearing the tables in the mess hall and I noticed a new man in the group. He looked to be in his late sixties. His face was weather-worn from years of sun and wind exposure. He stood about 6 feet tall, and when he looked at me, he looked so sad. I have seen this look in the eyes of many men at the mission. They have the eyes of regret. They try to cover it up with a gruff exterior, but way deep down, they are full of regret.

As I was clearing the tables, I thought I would take a moment to introduce myself to him. He was sitting in the back corner of the room all by himself. He had a small suitcase that I guessed carried all of his worldly possessions. As I walked up to him, he looked up and gave me a slight smile.

"My name is Sam," I said, and he reached out his hand and grunted, "Mike." I really didn't know what to say to him. This whole reaching out to others is a new thing to me. It's funny, in the past I would have said Poor Sap, hope he makes it—and then moved on. Now for some reason, I felt compelled to talk with him. I didn't know where to start, so I just started talking. I don't remember what I was talking about, and I don't think he really cared. He just looked at me and kept eating. Then I asked him where he was from. "All over," was all he said. "Oh," I said, "Me too." He stopped eating for a moment and then looked me in the eyes. It was almost unnerving. I kept talking, "What brings you here?" "Looking for a job," he replied. "Not many of those around here these days," I said.

Then for some reason, he started talking. Over the next few minutes, I just sat and listened to him. He told me of making huge dollars in the dot-com boom and then losing it all. He talked of all the extravagant homes and expensive cars he used to have and how it was all gone. He told me how, if he could do life over again, he would do it differently. This statement intrigued me. "What would you do differently?" I asked.

He looked at me for a moment, put his spoon on the table, wiped his mouth with a napkin, and leaned back in his chair. "Sam," he said, "I have lived a life that most would think was a success. In my field I was number one. I have traveled the world and worked with the best in the business. But if I could do it again, I'd be a janitor. I'd be home at nights with my family." Then he paused. His eyes got moist as he pondered his next sentence.

"Though I had everything that any man could want as far as material possessions, I lost the most important thing on this earth—my family. I was married to my job and to the idea of success. I was married to the business and the idea that came with all of the prestige of being the best. But in the end, now I am alone. Now I have lost everything. The houses, condos, boats, and cars. It's all gone."

I could tell it was hard for him to talk about his past so I apologized for bringing it up. He just smiled.

"No, Sam, it's fine. I've told this story to many men, mostly young guys, hoping they would learn from my mistakes."

We sat in a moment of silence just taking the moment in. Then he blurted out, "I have been diagnosed with cancer. I will be dead in less than a year."

I didn't know what to say. I just looked at him. He seemed to have a certain peace about it. "It's OK Sam," he said. "I have come to grips with the idea. My life is over. But yours is not. You may be nearing your last years here on this earth, but you have time. That is one thing that I wish I had more of. It's really the most valuable commodity in this world."

I shifted in my seat, and he could see that I was getting uncomfortable with the conversation. I've known for the past few weeks while spending time with Jason and being around his family that I needed to clear up the hurts of my past. I knew way deep down in my heart that I needed to find you, Kathleen, before it was too late. Looking at Mike I could tell that he knew he had touched something deep within me.

He straightened up in his chair and looked me in the eye. I could tell by his gaze that at one time in his life he was a man with power and authority. At this moment, he was a leader who demanded respect when he spoke.

"Sam," he said, "I can tell by looking into your eyes that there is something you need to do. Let me tell you something, if you don't do it now, you will regret it. Have the courage to go after that thing in your heart and don't let go of it until you get it. You don't know how long you have before you leave this place. None of us do."

I leaned back in my chair for a moment. I will be honest with you. I was uncomfortable with this discussion. He was making me face the one thing that I feared the most—seeing you and being rejected by you.

Then he got stern with me. "What is it, Sam, that you know you must do? What is it that is the deepest desire in your heart?"

Now I was the one with moist eyes. His words were cutting into my soul with every syllable. I stood to my feet and started clearing the dishes. He lost contact with my eyes and leaned back in his chair.

"Do it, Sam. Do it while you still have time. There were so many things that I wanted to do...things that would have brought peace in my life. But I traded my peace for fear, and I regret it every day of my life. Don't be like me, Sam. You still have time. Have the courage to do it. Do it now."

I just stared at him as the words came out of his mouth. As he spoke, all I could think of was seeing you again. I thanked him for the advice and got out of there as quickly as I could. But I knew he was right.

That night I went up to my room and as I lay on my bed staring at the ceiling I thought about what Mike had said. I thought about all of the possibilities and decided that I had to do it. I had to take a chance and find you.

So now I have started on my way to find you. It has been so long that I didn't know where to start. But just making the decision to do it lifted a tremendous weight from me. Jason has told me over and over again that a journey starts with the first step. You will never go anywhere unless you are willing to take the first step. Then the second and then the third until you reach your destination. Taking that first step was the hardest for me but now I am on my journey and it brings all sorts of feelings from great joy to great fear.

Kathleen, the next gift I want to give you is the *Gift of Courage* so you can live your life to the fullest. When you leave this world, I hope you leave it with no unfulfilled dreams.

Mike taught me a very valuable lesson that night. We all have dreams, and many times we do not go after them because we are afraid. We are afraid of failure or making a mistake. We are afraid of what others may think of us. I can tell you now that living the life I have lived was a life filled with mistakes. Everyone makes mistakes. The great thing about it, though, is that you can start over every day. Each and every day is a new opportunity to try again. If you learn from a mistake, then it is not a mistake. It is a life lesson. Jason told me that the only time you ever fail is when you give up. All the experiences that people may say were a failure is a learning experience—unless you let it beat you and you give up.

What I learned from that conversation with Mike is that it is better to live a life where you have the courage to put your fears aside at least once and try than to always wonder what would have happened if you had actually done it.

I don't know what your dreams are, Katy, but my desire is for you to go after them. Don't let any type of fear stop you from fulfilling your dreams. Don't be like me, running from one fear to another. Have the courage to face whatever brings fear to you and conquer it.

Kathleen—a life of courage.

*Restored*

# March 13, Legacy

Oretown, Oregon

It has been almost a month since my last entry. After my meeting with Mike, I decided it was time for me to find you. I went to the local library and the librarian helped me find you on the Internet. It looks like you now live in Tulsa, Oklahoma. I left Washington a few weeks back to head your way. First, I have to go south. I have some business in San Diego that I must take care of before I make my way East. So now I am walking and hitchhiking my way down the coast.

It has been pretty good going overall. I have met some nice people along the way. Yesterday, I was able to cover about 100 miles with a young man who was going from Portland to Oretown, Oregon. He had family there and was headed home for the weekend.

It's funny how things happen when you are traveling. I told him a little about my conversation with Mike, and how I was on the greatest journey of my life, and how I am going to make decisions so I have no regrets. I think, in a way, I was able to inspire him a little. It amazes me how just sharing some words with someone can give me a good feeling inside. I have never experienced this before.

He dropped me off once we reached town, and he said he was going to go after his dream— no regrets, no fear. I have to tell you, it brought a big smile to my face. This was the first time in a long time that I was able to inspire someone. It felt good.

I ate a quick meal at the local diner and met a lovely waitress named Marlene. She told me about a small Bed and Breakfast down the road that had very reasonable rates for wanderers like me. I walked down the road, and it led to a very quaint house right across the street from the beach.

The owner, Miss Esther, told me that there were no vacant rooms for that night, but there was a cot in the room above the garage that I could have for $5 a night. I agreed and thanked her. I think I may have scared her a little, as it had been a few days since I had had a good shave. I tend to look a little scary when I have stubble on my face—nowadays it's almost all white.

The room is nice—an open area with a small bathroom with a shower. After a shower and a shave, I walked on the beach. The sun was setting and there was a nice breeze coming off the water.

The beach was beautiful. I can't remember the last time I walked along the ocean and took in its entire splendor. There were huge boulders and sand dunes, and the water was cool with 3- to 4-foot waves crashing onto the beach. I forgot how much I enjoyed the beach. I saw all sorts of markings in the sand and realized they were tracks from all kinds of animals and birds that live here. I saw crab tracks, bird tracks, and snail trails. It was funny to me because even though I hadn't been along the coast for such a long time, I could still tell the difference between the tracks of the different creatures.

A little farther down, I saw more bird tracks. I knew they were sandpiper and puffin tracks by the shape and the pattern they left behind in the sand. I also knew because I watched the birds and noticed how they walked and how they kind of skipped across the sand. The marks they left in the sand were very distinct.

Looking at all the tracks in the sand made me start to think. Our lives are a lot like this beach— our hearts are like a beach. When we interact with other people, we leave a mark or tracks in their lives. These tracks are written on their hearts and souls. Many times people never forget the tracks you leave on their hearts, good or bad.

The tracks that we leave in the lives of other people are based on our experience with them— how we talk with one another, how we respect or disrespect them. Do we care about their wants, needs, or desires or do we just care about our own? I know in my life that I left a lot of bad tracks in many of the lives that I came across. My life was about me. All I cared about was what I wanted. I never took into account the needs of those around me.

I thank God that I am now able to see that there is a hope, that these relationships can be mended and the tracks on the hearts of those I have hurt can be brushed clean and new tracks can be made.

Time can be a lot like the waves. Each time a wave comes in, the track is washed away a little. After enough waves, the tracks are wiped away completely and the mark is gone. Time is like that, too. After enough time, people can heal, but if I walk on that beach again, I will leave those same tracks and cause the same pain. The only difference between people and the sand is that people will not let you back in their hearts to do the same damage again. Don't be fooled by time. It may seem like the pain is gone, but deep down the tracks are still there.

Grace and forgiveness is like a gentle summer rain. If you make things right with the person that you wronged, a gentle rain can come along and wipe the beach clean. This is that gentle rain that comes with forgiveness. It comes down and cleanses the beach wiping it clean so you can have another chance to walk the beach again.

Many times we don't know the type of tracks we are leaving until we return to the people and see the marks left on their hearts. You will know when you see them and notice how they talk to you or treat you.

I heard someone say once that you can tell what kind of tree you have in your yard by the kind of leaves it drops. A maple tree only drops maple leaves; oak trees drop oak leaves.

A maple tree cannot drop an oak leaf. Many people may say they are an oak tree, but the trail of leaves they leave behind them will tell the truth of what kind of tree they are. Just like the beach, you will know who they really are by the tracks they leave on your heart. Others will know who you really are by the tracks you leave on their heart.

In this journey of life, we walk our own individual path. When we interact with people, we leave tracks on their hearts. The type of track you leave determines who you truly are. We may walk around this world thinking we are one type of person; but if we take the time to really look at our tracks, we may see that we are someone else entirely.

Now I want to be a person who leaves behind the tracks of a kind person who has experienced forgiveness and has had the chains of guilt broken from my life. I want my tracks to leave a soft, forgiving, and loving impression on the heart of everyone I meet.

Kathleen, what I think I am talking about here is a legacy. Another thing I have learned is that all people leave behind a legacy. That legacy is the memories that others will have of you when you are gone. What that legacy is and how it affects others is up to us. I know that I have made many bad decisions, and I have left behind a lot of bad tracks in the lives of those I have encountered, but I also know that there is a grace and a forgiveness that allows me to brush away the bad tracks and create new tracks.

My next gift for you is the *Gift of a Legacy*— that you learn the value of the lives of those around you. I hope that you realize how important every life is and that you leave a mark on every person you meet. I hope that you leave behind a legacy of grace in the lives of those whose beach you had the pleasure to walk on.

# April 5, Giving

## Gold Beach, Oregon

*W*ell, here I am in Gold Beach, Oregon. I spent the last couple of weeks with Miss Esther—the owner of the Oretown Family Inn—the Bed and Breakfast that I had planned on staying only for the night. Once she saw me cleaned up a little, I guess I didn't scare her so much. I had noticed some damage on the spouting coming off the roof of the house, so I told her I could help her out with it and she was grateful. After that, she asked if I could help with a sticky window, and then I was a painter, landscaper, and carpenter.

Miss Esther was a wonderful lady. She had golden brown skin that made me think of caramel and chocolate mixed together. Originally from Georgia via the "whole world," she told me she moved to Oretown about five years ago because it was her husband's dream to retire in Oregon and run a B and B. He died last year, and she has been running the place by herself ever since. She didn't complain. According to her, "There's always something to be thankful for."

She was an amazing person. She told me of stories of traveling the world with her husband, "Mr. Frank." The two were always looking for adventure. Always expecting something good to happen. When she would make these statements, it seemed strange to me. This was a new way of thinking for me. I guess in my life, I had always expected bad things to happen. And looking back, it looks like I got what I expected.

One night while we were sitting on the porch watching the sun set over the ocean, she told me about her first trip to India. It was almost 40 years ago. While there, she and her husband met a young couple in the city of Hyderabad. The couple had moved to India for work— during those days, there was a big demand in the technology field. Unfortunately, the job had gone away and they were stranded there. They wanted to stay because they really liked India, but he couldn't find work. Because they were American, they could only work for an American company with offices in India. Unable to find a job, they now had to look for a place to stay each night.

Miss Esther said that her husband took the young man aside to have a talk with him. As they walked away, Miss Esther knew something was up. She tried to cheer up the young lady, but she couldn't keep her eyes off of Frank, she knew he was up to something. She saw Frank reach into his pocket, take out the last of their cash, and give it to the young man.

Miss Esther told me, "Now you have to understand son, this was before the days of automatic tellers and the such. I knew we didn't have any more cash, but I trusted that Frank knew what he was doing...and I knew the good Lord would take care of us.

"You should have seen the look on that boy's face when my husband handed him the money! He tried to push it back, but my husband could be a very persuasive man when he wanted to be. Those two couldn't stop thanking us. There were hugs all around, and then they were on their way. We still keep in touch." Then she pointed through the window into the house. "That's them right there." On the table was a picture of a nice-looking family with four grown children and it looked to be about a dozen grandchildren.

"You see, Sam. It's better to give than it is to receive. Frank was a planter. He sowed all kinds of seeds in the lives of those around him. He knew that the good Lord would some day bring him a harvest. I must say, even today I'm still reaping a harvest of good things because of the seeds he sowed."

We paused for a moment looking at the water just as the sun sunk below the horizon. And then there was a flash of green light.

"Wow, I've never seen that before," I said.

"Just the Lord saying 'Goodnight, Sam.'"

Before we went inside, I just had to ask her the question burning in my mind.

"How did you get home from India if you gave all your cash away?"

She just chuckled at the question. "I don't rightly remember. All I know is…whenever we needed something, it was always there."

Then she stood up and said, "Come with me, I want to show you something." We walked into the house through the dining room and into the study. She walked over to a shelf on which was an oil lamp. It looked to be a couple hundred years old at least. She reached up and picked it up using both hands. She stared at it for a moment. Then she looked at me, "We got this lamp on that trip and it changed our lives."

Then she handed it to me. I held it carefully for a moment not really knowing what to do with it. She then pointed to the side and asked, "Can you tell me what it says on this side of the lamp?"

I held the lamp up and studied it. I had to put my glasses on to read the inscriptions. On one side there were some symbols that I didn't understand. It looked like old Egyptian writing. On the other side there was a phrase in English. When I paused, she prodded, "Can you tell me what it says on that side of the lamp, Sam?"

"Oh yes, let me see." I had to get in the light so I could read it. "A life worth living is not determined by what is gotten, rather by what is given." As I looked back up at her, she grew a big smile, "Well, I'll be," she said.

I asked what she meant by that. She just smiled and said, "The Lamp says different things to different people. I always wondered what that side said. Thank you for coming here and reading it to me."

That night I laid in my bed thinking about our conversation and what she said. It was time for me to move on. I had made enough money working for Miss Esther to have a little pocket change and enough to buy a bus ticket. The nearest Greyhound station was in Salem, about 50 miles east.

The next morning I gave Miss Esther a big hug and said my good-byes. It was a bittersweet time for me. I am sure I will never forget her. I caught a ride with Marlene, the waitress from the diner. She was driving to Salem to pick up supplies for the restaurant.

When we arrived in Salem, I got out at the station and thanked her for the ride. I purchased my ticket. I only had enough money to get as far as Redding, California. As I sat in the waiting area, I saw a young family come into the station. There was a man and woman and their four children, who all looked to be under about 7 years old. The youngest was a baby. I couldn't help but notice the large family. They walked straight up to the counter to purchase their tickets. Then for a moment the conversation got kind of loud. I wasn't sure what was going on, but I could tell the wife was very upset. Then she and the children came over and sat by me while her husband was having a serious discussion with the bus agent.

After a couple of moments I asked her if everything was OK. She looked up at me with tears in her eyes. "Everything is fine, thanks for asking." Then she returned to tending to her baby. A few moments later her husband walked over. I could hear him talking with his wife.

"They say there is nothing they can do. We will have to come back tomorrow and catch the next one," he said.

His wife didn't want to hear that. "What if she dies tonight, then what? I want my children to see their grandmother before she dies…and I know you want to say good-bye to your mother," she said.

They went on talking for a while and then I did something that I have never done before. I got involved in another person's life—to help them. I had gotten involved in other's lives in the past if it was to my benefit, but this was the first time I felt compelled to help someone else. I guess the conversation with Miss Esther and the inscription on that lamp made an impression on me.

"Excuse me, I don't mean to eavesdrop on your conversation, but is there something that I can do to help?"

"Not unless you want to give up your seat," the young mother said. She explained how her husband's mother was in a bad car accident and the doctor didn't think she would make it through the night. They needed to get to Redding today. Their car was in no shape to make the long trip, and they couldn't afford plane tickets on such short notice. Taking the bus was the only way, but there were only five seats left. They could hold the baby on her lap, but they still needed one more seat.

"So please don't take this the wrong way... but unless you are willing to give up your seat, there is really nothing you can do," she said.

I was faced with an opportunity to give. It would cause an inconvenience for me because I was on my way to see you, but for some reason, I knew you would understand. In the past, I would have brushed off the woman's comment with a "sucks to be you" attitude. Heck, I wouldn't have even talked to them. And now I was faced with the choice to give up my seat so they could go home to be with their dying mother and grandmother.

What could I do? I had to do it. So I did!

"All right then," I said.

"All right then what?" she asked.

"You can have my seat. I would be happy to give it to you." I'll be honest with you, I didn't expect what followed after that. She handed off the baby right quick and grabbed me around the neck and squeezed so hard I thought I was going to lose consciousness. She kissed me on the cheek.

"Mister, you don't know what this means to us. Thank you, thank you, thank you!"

We exchanged names and gave a few more hugs and then they were on their way. I walked down to the local shelter to catch a bed before they were filled up.

Kathleen, my next gift to you is the *Gift of Giving*.

I didn't realize the power that is packed in that one simple act of giving. One thing I learned from Miss Esther is that the seeds you plant today will be the harvest you reap tomorrow. The seeds you plant determine the things you want or what you want to happen in your life in the years to come. Plant seeds of love and understanding in other people's lives today. The way you want to be treated in the future is how you should treat others today.

Giving doesn't always have to be money. For some it's time, for others it's words. It can be whatever is needed at that moment. Jason read a verse in the Bible that says, "Give and it shall be given to you. Pressed down, shaken together, and running over will men give back to you."

Kathleen—learn to have the heart of a giver. That's where you will find true peace in your life. Those who are takers are never satisfied. They always want more—I know. It's the givers who find a real place of satisfaction in their lives.

Just as written on that old oil lamp, "A life worth living is not determined by what is gotten, rather by what is given."

# Restored

## April 30, Freedom

### San Francisco, California

*W*ell here I am in San Francisco. I spent about two weeks in Redding because I picked up some work at the mission working in the kitchen. I looked around town for work as soon as I got in, but again, I can look a little scary to some folks before I get cleaned up. So I went to the local mission to see if I could get a bed for the night. As I walked in, there was a man greeting people at the door. Unfortunately, he was turning people away since they were full for the night. As I approached, he said that there were no more beds available, unless I was willing to work. I quickly said, "Yes sir, ready, willing, and able." So I got a job in the kitchen washing dishes again. I must be pretty good at it because I keep finding myself in the position.

It made me think of some of the things that Jason used to say to me. He told me that if I trusted the Lord, He would provide for all of my needs. That didn't mean I could just sit back and wait for God to hand me things. I need to look for opportunities and He would guide me to a way to fulfill my need. I think that happened in Redding when I got the job. I needed a bed and money so I could buy another bus ticket to get closer to you.

I have never been to San Francisco before, so one afternoon I thought I would take a walk around town. It was a very interesting place. I had seen pictures of all these things before, but to see them in real life was amazing. I went down to Fisherman's Wharf and bought seafood in a cup. They call it walk-away shrimp. Then I rode a trolley car up the hill to see the twisted road. I can't remember the name of it right now. From there I could see Coit Tower. I caught the trolley back down the hill and went to the beach area, where I could see the Golden Gate Bridge. It was a spectacular sight.

It was late afternoon and the sun was still warm. There were several families on the beach, and there were even swimmers doing laps along the shore. I took a shoe off and put my toe in. It was too cold for me. I walked up and down the beach for a while and soaked in the sights.

As I was walking along, I noticed a man and his young daughter. She must have been 2 or 3 years old. They were walking along the edge of the water where every third wave or so would be about 8 inches deep. The little girl would squeal with delight and run up the shore to dry land. Her dad would stop and wait for her to come back to him and they continued walking.

Along the way, the little girl started to pick up some small stones. It was really cute how each stone was like a treasure. She showed each to her dad and he examined them, telling her how beautiful they were. She smiled and then searched for another.

I couldn't stop watching them because it was such a nice time for them—and I thought how happy you would have been if I had strolled along the shore with you all those years ago. I'm sorry, Kathleen, for not sharing this kind of special time with you.

This little girl was determined to find as many treasures as she could. After awhile, both hands were full and she was cupping them against her tummy to be able to hold them all. Her father kept examining and approving the stones as she collected more. She was having a hard time carrying them, and now she had some tucked under her chin and she was holding her shirt like a basket.

And then it happened. She saw a beautiful blue stone—a big one. You could tell by the look in the little girl's eyes that this was the most beautiful rock she had ever seen. It was about 10 inches across and a deep blue with what looked like a white granite stripe through the middle of it. The little girl stopped, bent over, and tried to pick up the beautiful blue rock. But because her hands were so full, she was having a difficult time. She tried shifting the stones to one side and they spilled out. She shifted to the other side and out they fell. She started getting frustrated and started to whine about her predicament. I could hear her father talking with her softly.

"Josey, if you want that big rock, you will have to let go of the other stones you are holding." She didn't like that idea. She had amassed quite a collection and did not want to let it go. She started to cry, and her father said, "Let's go. Leave the rock and be happy with the stones you already have."

I laughed watching her. She was such a determined little thing and she wanted that big rock and all the others. They started to walk away, but all of a sudden she stopped and turned back.

She walked back to the rock and dropped all of the smaller stones she was carrying. Then she bent over and picked up the beautiful blue rock. She got the biggest smile on her face, let out a yelp, and ran back to her father. "Look, Daddy… rock." Now she was happy. They kept walking and I enjoyed the moment.

As I walked back up the beach toward the road, I had a thought. During my life I was just like that little girl. I always held on to a dream that I wanted to fulfill, but issues in my past held me back or caused me to give up. To realize a dream in my life, I know now that I have to let go of some of the things I was holding on to. I was just like the little girl with her collection of stones she had picked up along the way—or should I say, the beach of life. Then on her journey she came across what she really wanted—something that would fulfill her to that point. But she had to let go of all the little things from her past that were stopping her from picking up the big, beautiful rock. She had no room in her life for the one thing she really wanted. She had to be willing to let go.

Kathleen, we are all the same in this manner. In our walk along the beach of life we pick up stones along the way—stones of comfort, blame, fear, security, good enough, compromise, and of giving up.

To get to where we really want to be in our lives, to realize the dream that has been in our hearts for most of our lives, we may have to take a look at what is in our hands—what are we holding on to. What stones have we collected? What things are we carrying that prevent us from picking up the one thing we really want? After you see what you've been holding on to, then you will have to decide which stones you are willing to give up to achieve your dreams.

Jason often told me that the thing that holds most people back is the fear of failing. He said for many it is crippling, and the crazy thing about that—in most cases, if people would face it and go after what they fear, they most often beat it. The first step to overcoming fear is just taking that first step.

Jason said that the biggest mistake people make is to not do anything because they do not want to make a mistake. I wrote about mistakes in a previous journal entry, but it's important to realize that everyone makes mistakes. Hopefully, along the way we learn how not to make the same mistakes. Don't let fear of failure or fear of making a mistake stop you from pursuing your dreams. Throw the fear stone deep into the ocean—right next to the giving-up stone. Throw both of them deep into the ocean.

We all have dreams, wants, and desires. There is something in the back of our minds or way deep in our hearts that keeps nudging us. Maybe it's one of those dreams that we have shared with a few people but haven't realized yet. Maybe because it seems too big or too far away. Maybe it seems impossible because we don't have the right training or background. Maybe we were told as a kid by a parent or someone we looked up to that we couldn't do it.

Maybe for you Katy, because I left when you were young, you blame yourself and your self-esteem isn't where it should be. I'm sorry, Katy. But, somehow your dream is still there. The wonder of it still excites you. The "If only I could try, I think I could do it." You feel it every day, but nothing happens.

For me, up until a few months ago, the stones filling my hands were the stones of complacency. I thought that I lived my life and this is the lot that I had drawn for the rest of my life. I sacrificed my family to get what I thought would make me happy. I traded true happiness for material possessions and now I have neither. But I do have a new dream, and that is to see you again and ask your forgiveness.

Jason said that all things are possible if I would only believe. If I really wanted to find you, I would find a way to do it. I have found that the more I tell others of my dream, the more support I get and the more I realize it can happen. I guess this is called faith.

I will be honest with you. Letting go of the stones of my past has been very hard. Every day I remember the hurt that I caused you and many other people. But now I have this newfound faith that if I truly believe, anything is possible. That there can be a happy ending to my life.

Kathleen, please take a moment and look way deep into your heart. What is that unrealized dream you have? Maybe it's a better position at your workplace. Maybe it's a different job entirely. Maybe you want a deeper relationship with your husband or children. Maybe you want to make a positive difference in your community in some way. Maybe you want to see me—I hope that is so.

Then look into your hands to see what stones you have collected over the years. See which stones do not work with your dream. Then throw them deep into the ocean. Drop them like hot pieces of coal. Get rid of them as fast as you can. Make room for the big, beautiful, blue rock. Start walking down the beach and find that perfect rock. Bend down and pick it up. You will be amazed at how things will line up for you once you start working toward your dream. I remember a quote I heard once from Thomas Jefferson, he said, "I find the harder I work, the more lucky I become." I now believe this is true. When you work toward a goal and you focus on that goal, you will see things differently and you will start to notice opportunities in your life that help you with your dream that you never noticed before.

As you work toward your dream, you will find that it will be easy and natural for you because you have made room in your life for the rock. All the stones are where they belong and you have room to carry the rock.

As you learn to do this, it will become second nature to you. After you carry that rock for a while, you may find another rock, and then one day you might see a boulder off in the distance, and you will want to pick it up. That will be OK, because you won't be carrying a lap full of rocks to get in the way of the boulder you want to carry. Like the little girl on the beach with her dad, enjoy searching for stones and rocks and boulders, but know when they are holding you back from greater opportunities.

Kathleen, my next gift to you is the *Gift of Freedom*—freedom from your past and freedom for your future.

Come to the realization that you can be free to do anything you want and you can become anyone you want to be. Don't let the issues of the past hold you back from achieving your future. Find that one thing way deep down inside you that you feel would define you as a person and go after it. Realizing along the way that you are free to do and be whoever you want to be.

## May 5, Family

### San Francisco, California

I'm still in San Francisco. I have been working at the mission. It is run by a guy named Brother Ron, that is what he asks us to call him; has been good to me. He moved me out of the kitchen and into the recreation area. I hand out books, ping-pong paddles, and other items for the men staying there. It is strange how in some offbeat way, Brother Ron and some of these guys have become like family to me. In group meetings, we spend a lot of time together talking and listening to each other, and that's when I think that I have built this unique bond with them.

A couple of days ago, I called Jason in Seattle. It was good to hear his voice again. He wanted to know all about my travels. When I told him I was in San Francisco, he said that he was coming to San Francisco on business and wanted to have lunch. I was excited about seeing my good friend.

When Jason came in town, we met at the mission. I gave him the grand tour and we spent a little time with Brother Ron. Come to find out, they were good friends. It was like two brothers who hadn't seen each other in a long time. The two of them are a lot alike. After meeting with Ron, we took a trolley car ride past the crooked road, which I learned is named Lombard Street. You need to see this street—it is the curviest street I've ever seen. We got off the trolley at the bottom of the hill and walked over to the wharf. Jason had never had walk-away shrimp before, so I was happy to introduce him to this fine dining experience.

We walked up the street and found a nice table to sit and eat our lunch. He didn't waste any time asking me questions. He wanted to know all about my trip so far. I told him about Miss Esther and what I learned from her about giving. I also told him about the Robinson family that I met at the bus station and how I experienced the joy of giving. Jason and I had a great time. He was so happy for me.

Then I told him about the little girl and her daddy that I saw on the beach the other day. I told him about the stones and how I saw things differently after that experience. He said, "Sam, your spirit is alive now. Your whole life is going to be different. You will see everything in a new light."

I didn't really know what to think about his "your spirit is alive now" comment. But it's true—I do see things differently. I see life lessons everywhere I go. I'm not really looking for them; they just seem to appear to me now.

I went on to tell him how hard it was for me to watch that daddy and little girl on the beach because it made me think of you and how I was not there in your life to teach you the important life lessons. Just talking with him about it brought a tear to my eye. I didn't realize until these past couple of days how much pain I have been carrying around with me all of these years.

"Sam," Jason said, "most men don't realize that the most valuable gift in the world is other people. So many times people strive to accomplish things or to own things, and in the end when it's all said and done, if you don't have someone to share it with, it was all for nothing."

As I sat listening to him, I realized that I was the perfect example of what he was talking about. It made me think back over 25 years ago when I left the house that Christmas Eve, it was the hardest thing I have ever done. You may think that I was just being selfish and that I didn't care for you—well, you are right about the selfish part. But I did care for you, I loved you very much. In my own warped sense of reasoning, I thought that what I was doing would be better for you than having me around. In the state I was in, I'm sure that would have been true in the long run.

You see, I grew up in a bad situation with my father. He was a drinker and a womanizer for as long as I can remember. For the life of me I can't understand why my mother stayed with him all those years. I can remember as a child, times when she would be in her room crying all by herself over something that he had done. He ended up drinking himself to death. He died when I was 14 of liver failure. The only memories I have of him are sad. I guess more for my mother than anything else. He left her with nothing but sadness...and me.

As I got older I remember saying to myself that I was going to be nothing like him. I was going to be different. I was going to have money and buy nice things for my family. So when I met your mother, that's what I promised her. I told her that I would give her a life with no lack. I would work hard and get her everything she could ever want.

We started dating in high school. I was 15 and she was 14. I remember the first time I saw her. She was the most beautiful girl in the whole school. It was all over. I was whipped from the beginning.

We had been dating for about 3 years. I was getting ready to graduate high school. We both had big plans for our lives. I was going to go to college and get a business degree and start my own business. Your mother wanted to be a cosmetologist. We were going to get married and live in the city and raise our family. Then one night I went to pick her up for a date and she was sitting up in her room. I went up there to get her moving, and she had the most serious look on her face. "Al (that is what they called me then)," she said and then paused. Then she began to cry.

"What is it, are you OK?" I didn't know what to think, I had never seen her like this. "Did someone die? What's going on?" I still remember this moment just like it was yesterday. She had her face in her hands and she was weeping. "Please tell me what's wrong," I yelled at her.

"I'm pregnant," she said.

Those words changed my life forever. Pregnant. In those days, it was not acceptable to be unwed and pregnant, let alone being a teenager. This would be a huge disgrace to the family. So in our wisdom, we planned to get married. It was the right thing to do. After all, I loved her. At least I thought I knew what love was at the time.

We thought it best to hide it for as long as we could, but it was coming to the time where she was beginning to show. We thought about running away and getting married in Las Vegas but we didn't have the money to do that. The time came where we would have to tell her parents. She was working at the grocery store as a cashier and she worked until 9 P.M., so I picked her up after work and we drove to her parents' house.

We didn't talk much. I guess we really didn't know what to say. When we arrived at her house, we thought it would be best to tell them right away. We all sat down in the living room, and to this day I think your grandmother knew what was going on from the moment we walked through the front door. When she looked at your mom, she had an all-knowing look on her face. I suppose it didn't help that your mother couldn't look her in the face. I think she knew for some time, but didn't want to let it be a reality.

Your grandmother cried as your mother told her the news. She basically turned her back on your mother. She felt that she had brought disgrace to the family. On the other hand, your grandfather actually took it quite well. He took me into the other room to have "a little talk." He told me that he was disappointed and that he expected a lot more from me. He also told me that I would marry his daughter and take her somewhere where no one knew her to have the baby.

I graduated the next month and we got married at the courthouse. It was me, your mother, her parents, and my mom. Not the fairy-tale wedding I think she was dreaming of.

Per your grandfather's instructions, I looked for a job outside of town. I found one at a grain mill in Forest Lake, so our honeymoon was spent looking for an apartment. We found a small place just outside of town. It was about 40 minutes from where your grandparents lived. At the time, that didn't seem far enough away for me. But your mother wanted to be closer. She wanted to mend the relationship with her parents. I just wanted to hide from them.

I worked a lot at the mill to save as much money as I could. This was the beginning of the end for me, as I knew my chances of success in the corporate world were gone. I was loading trucks with grain sacks to take care of my pregnant wife.

Three months after we moved to Forest Lake, you came along. You were the most beautiful baby I had ever seen. It amazed me how the arrival of a new life can soften the hearts of people. When your grandmother held you in her arms, she melted with love. She wanted to see you all the time. We kept getting invites to come stay the weekend at their house. Your grandfather even offered to put in a good word for me at his office. Of course, my pride kept me from accepting the offer; I refused any help. I was going to do this on my own.

I wanted to get out of the apartment and into a house as soon as possible. I worked extra shifts at the mill. After a couple of years, I had become one of their best employees. I was a hard worker and became quite knowledgeable about the mill operations. I was promoted to shift supervisor, and soon after that, I became plant manager. The owners liked my dedication and drive. I worked whenever they needed me. Nights, weekends, holidays, it didn't matter. If they needed me, I was there.

I'm sorry to say that as I advanced at work, I went backward at home. Your mother was spending more and more time with her parents in St. Paul. And I just worked more and more. Then, in about our third year of marriage, I was promoted and offered a job at the head-quarters just outside of St. Paul. I accepted the job, thinking that this move would help heal our marriage. I figured the extra income would make life easier.

The demands of corporate life got stronger with the new position. I started drinking at night to calm my nerves. This did not sit well with your mother. She started telling me that I was becoming my father. I knew it was true, but I wouldn't admit it. The fights got stronger and stronger. By the time you were 8 years old, I was in and out of the house on a regular basis. I started seeing other women who "understood" me better.

The truth I did not want to admit was, I *had* become my father. Your mother begged me to quit the job and take something less stressful. She said she didn't need the big house or the cars. She just wanted me. This was like speaking a foreign language to me. Why wouldn't she want the nicer things in life? I thought I had done well for myself considering where I had come from. I had a good, high-paying job, a large house, and nice cars. What else did she need?

Over the next couple of years we grew more and more distant from one another. I kept taking any assignment that would take me out of town. I drank regularly and depending on how bad our fight was, I found other companions who understood what I was dealing with. Then, that fateful Christmas Eve when you were ten, I left.

I had become my father. How could it be true? The very person I hated and blamed for my problems. How could I be just like him?

I will never forget that night. We had another of our knock-down, drag-out fights. I had enough; I was going to leave for good. I thought you were in bed. I stormed out the front door and down the driveway. Then out of nowhere, I heard a knock on the window. I stopped and turned around. I really didn't expect to see you. There you were in the window looking at me with those pleading eyes. You ripped a hole through my heart. I didn't know what to do, so I turned and just kept walking. This started a new pattern in my life. I just kept walking.

Kathleen—I want you to know that it was not your fault that I left. It was mine. I put value in all the wrong things. I put more value in the house and cars and prestige of the titles and money than I did you or your mother. I thought all of that stuff was what would define me, but now I know the truth. The truth that people are all that really matter in life. Family and friends.

Kathleen, my next gift for you is the *Gift of Family*. It is my prayer that you will have an understanding that love and family are more valuable than any possession.

I wasted a whole life carrying around hurts and pains from a past that I blamed other people for only to realize at the end of my life that I was wrong. I was wrong to blame your mother, wrong to blame your grandfather, and wrong to give up.

If I had it to do all over again, I would have swallowed my pride and realized that I didn't have to be right in every situation. I would have put my family above all my desires for material things.

I don't know where you are with your family. I don't know if you have a family. All I know is that you will find true happiness only by loving and being loved.

Kathleen—The greatest gift in life is the gift of family. Learn to embrace them and work through any differences that may drive you apart. Learn that without them you are all alone in the world. We all need others to survive and to be whole. It took me a lifetime to learn this. Please learn it now.

## May 7, Creativity

San Francisco, California

Jason was in town for a couple more days. He does a lot of awareness speeches for the mission organization that he works with. I did not know this, but he comes from a very wealthy family. He has funded the mission in Seattle with his own money for the past five years. He was actually in town raising money for the mission that I was working in. According to Brother Ron, Jason had inherited a fortune from his grandfather and he has been working to give it all away. He said Jason's grandfather made him do a bunch of exercises over a year before he would give him the money. He said the money was a great gift, but the lessons Jason learned from his grandfather were the Ultimate Gift.

He had a meeting with a man who owned a large company and he invited me to come along. At first, I didn't know what to think. I thought that he might be using me to persuade the man to give money to the mission.

It's funny where your mind can go sometimes. I mean, Jason has done nothing but help me, and when this opportunity came to help him, I automatically thought that he was using me. Just shows how we always have to check our motives. Jason always says that, "if we get offended by what others do, it's because we are only being concerned with ourselves. If I'm looking out for my fellow man, how can someone offend me?" That's a good question. So I got past my selfishness and told him that I would be happy to go along with him. I dug out my best clothes—a pair of jeans, a vest, and my bolo tie.

He picked me up in the morning, and we drove downtown. Their offices were at the top of one of the glass skyscrapers. It had been years since I had been in the corporate environment. It brought back some strange feelings. The sad truth of it all is that when I was in the corporate environment I was a bulldog. I was the guy they gave the tough assignments to because they knew I would do whatever it took to get it done—work the long hours and stab anyone in the back if I had to.

During the ride up in the elevator, Jason was humming a little tune to himself. He had a big smile on his face. I was surprised at how calm he seemed to be. I asked him if he ever got nervous at these meetings. He said not really. He believed that his steps were guided and that he was just walking out the path laid before him. If this meeting were to be fruitful it was because the Lord had made a way. I asked what he meant by that. He said that he felt the work he was doing was what God had asked him to do. He believed that his steps were guided by God and that he just had to go where he felt God was telling him to go.

"If the money for the mission is to come from this place, then it will," Jason said. "If not, God will bring it from somewhere else. If the money doesn't come in at all, then the mission will go away. I can only do what I believe He is leading me to do. I can't make the mission the goal; I will always reach out to people. If not through the mission, then another way. God will tell me what to do." Then he smiled and went back to humming.

I have to tell you, I had never heard anything like that before. This man had a faith like I had never seen before in my life. Not only did he believe what he was saying, he lived it.

We stopped at the 47th floor and got off the elevator into a grand entrance. This was an architectural firm. There were pictures and blueprints of different buildings all over the walls. There were also small building models on tables. I recognized many of the buildings from different cities all over the country. We were asked to wait for a few moments, so we sat in the leather and chrome chairs in the reception area.

After about five minutes, we were led into a very large, well-furnished office with a huge mahogany conference table and matching desk. Sitting behind the desk was the owner of the firm, James Horst. He stood as we walked in and came around the desk to meet us. Jason shook hands with him and then introduced me. I shook his hand and said, "Very nice to meet you, Mr. Horst."

He laughed and said, "Mr. Horst is my father, call me Jim." Jason and Jim had a chuckle, and then we all sat at the end of the conference table.

Jim started the conversation with a little small talk about the weather and then they got right to it.

"So Jason, what have you got for me this year?"

Jason started laying out his plans to expand the sleeping area of the mission so he could accommodate more people. Jim listened intently and nodded as Jason talked. Jason told him about all the good things going on at the mission and all of the lives being touched and changed. Jason talked for about 40 minutes as Jim listened. I was amazed at how much time Jason was getting with this man and how much respect he was giving Jason. I found myself staring at Jason and thinking how proud I was that he was my friend.

Jason finished his presentation and Jim took all of the materials. Then Jim turned to me and said, "This all looks and sounds great, but what I really want to know is what do you think, Sam?"

His question took me by surprise. I wasn't expecting to take part in the conversation. I was just going along to observe. "Well, sir..."

"Jim," he said.

"Ah, Jim. I have known Jason for some time now, and I know him to be an honest man who does what he says. I know he is doing a good work with the mission. To be honest, he changed my life."

Jim smiled and said, "Good enough for me, let's do it."

I was amazed. *Why does this man even care about this mission, let alone want to put hundreds of thousands of dollars into it?*

I had to know more about him. I said, "Jim, if you don't mind me asking, how did you get to where you are today?"

He paused for a moment, "If you have a little time, I would like to share my journey with you."

"Please do," I said.

He stood up and motioned for us to walk over to a couch and a couple of chairs in another part of his office. Then he started to talk. I'm going to try to write down everything he said as I remember it, so you can learn from him too, Katy.

"It all comes down to this. Who do you believe that you are? Because who you believe you are is who you will be."

I was a little confused by that statement and I think he could tell by the look on my face.

"Are you a man of faith, Sam? Do you believe in your Creator?" "Yes, now I do," I said. "I mean recently in the past few months, Jason here has introduced me to the whole concept."

"Good, because that is where the basis of what I'm going to share with you comes from. You see, Sam, we are all created in the image of our Creator. This means that we are beings who were created to create. The important thing to understand is that we are all creating all of the time. We are always in a state of creation. Every time you have a thought, you are creating. That is where it all starts. There is a good side and a bad side to that. Good thoughts create good things and bad thoughts create bad things."

Then Jim pointed to his head, "This is where it all starts—right here in your head, with your thoughts. Everything that we are in this life is a result of our thinking. Our thinking leads us to what we say, and what we say is what we believe and act on. What we act on is what we create. You see, Sam, your life is a result of the choices and decisions that you have made up to this point. Where you are in your life right now, good or bad, is a direct result of the choices you made. Where you want to be in the future is based on the choices and decisions you start making today. If you don't like where your life is now, change it. How do you do that? Change your thinking."

Then Jim paused for a moment. He looked at both Jason and me. "Let's take a look at my life, for instance. You wouldn't know it now, but I was not a very positive person most of my life. I thought that other people always got the breaks and I never got a break—nothing was going right. I complained about everything and everyone. I was never happy no matter what the situation. I couldn't get a decent job, I wasn't happy with my marriage, and I couldn't see a way out.

"Then one day a coworker talked me into going to a lunch meeting with a speaker. I thought what the heck, it was a free lunch, right? Little did I know that free lunch would cost me my life as I knew it. That was OK; it wasn't really worth much at the time.

"The luncheon speaker was a Christian, and he told us how truths from the Bible could help us in our business. This was the first I had heard of that, so I was intrigued by him and what he had to say. I kept expecting him to pass the plate and raise some money. He never did; he broke it down for us. He talked about choice. He read a Scripture that God had set before us life and death and that He was allowing us to choose which way we go with it. The funny part is that the Scripture also said that God suggests we choose life.

"So again we are back to the point that we are beings created in the image and likeness of our Creator and we have the ability to create our lives. Our Creator suggests that we choose life. So how do we do that?"

I just stared at Jim and he said, "I'm glad you asked. We do it with our thoughts. The Bible says in the Book of Romans that we should not be like this world, but we should transform our lives. How do we do that? By renewing our minds. Everything starts with a thought. The Bible also says that we should take our thoughts captive. We should consider the things that we dwell on in our thought life. Measure it and decide if it can stay or go."

"Everything starts with a thought. Every invention first started out as a thought, and then someone spoke it into existence. They shared the idea with another person by using words. From there it goes on paper, or in today's world in a computer, and then it is shared with others until it becomes a reality, a tangible physical object. It all started with a thought.

"Our lives are just like that. What we need to understand is that we are creating our lives every day. First by the thoughts that we dwell on, which trigger the words we say, which become the basis for what we act on, which are the building blocks for our lives. We are building our lives every day. Most people think that their life is just a happenstance or a result of chance. Some people think that others are luckier than they are, that they get all the breaks. No, the fact is they have created their lives just like we all do—with our thoughts, words, and actions."

Kathleen, when I heard this, it changed my life. I realized that I was a complainer. That all the things I complained about were happening. I realized that I had created the life I had and that it was up to me to change it. So I did.

The first thing I did was choose to put good thoughts into my head every day. I read the Bible or books that had a positive message every day. I fed myself what I wanted my life to be. Then I broke off relationships that did not add to my life. Then I started saying things to and about myself that I wanted to have or be in my life.

I changed my thinking, words, and actions. This changed my life. The amazing thing is—all of a sudden I noticed that good things were happening to me. I was creating a life that I wanted.

I truly believe that God has given us the ability to create our lives. Good or bad.

Back to the meeting. At that point, Jim looked at us and smiled. I had never heard this way of thinking before so it took a moment for it to sink in. We said our good-byes and Jim walked with us to the lobby. Then he said, "Sam, here is one other thing that will help you create a great life. Give." He reached over to his assistant and she handed him a check. He looked at Jason and said, "I already had a check prepared for you before you came in. Keep up the good work."

Jason accepted the check and thanked him with a firm handshake. Then he just had to laugh. We rode the elevator down in silence. I had to digest all that was said in that meeting.

Kathleen, for some reason God has given me a second chance. I don't take that lightly. He is teaching me all of the things that I wish I would have known as a young man. That is why I have this burning desire to share them with you.

The next gift I have for you is the *Gift of Creativity*—and hope that you understand your creative ability in life.

Please don't take this lightly. It is important to realize that our lives are what they are because of what we believe. If you're not happy with where you are in your life, realize the creative ability you have and change your life—first with your thoughts, then your words, and then your actions.

Understand your true creative ability in life.

# July 7, Fearless

## San Francisco, California

A lot has happened over the past few months. I have been staying and working at the mission, and I have come to really enjoy it. I help out in all areas of the mission right now. I find the group sessions to be very rewarding. Last week I was able to share some of the information that I learned from my meeting with Jim and Jason. It amazes me how a little bit of truth in someone's life can turn on a light bulb and open all kinds of possibilities.

I was talking to the group about how the choices we make determine the life we have.

One of the guys who attended the session told me that he had never heard anything like that before. To understand that his life is where it is only because of the choices he has made in his life blew him away. Like this man and me, most people go through life thinking that they are where they are because of the cards they were dealt. They think that nothing can be done so they settle with what they have. To understand that we create our lives daily by our decisions, changes everything. It set this guy free—me too.

The funny thing about all this is that there were about 15 guys in this particular session and he was the only one who got excited about it. I don't know if the others got it or not, but this one guy sure did. I was happy to help him.

Last week Brother Ron called me into his office to have "a chat." I'll be honest with you, being called into an office for a chat did not excite me. In fact, it scared me. You have to understand Brother Ron. He is one of those guys who looks like a tough, gruff person. He stands over 6 feet tall and has a build like a football player. He works out in the rec center every day.

You can tell when you look in his eyes that he has had a lot of experience in his life. He is no stranger to trouble. His office is very unassuming. It has a simple, old wooden desk with a couple of file cabinets against the wall. He has a trophy on top of one of the cabinets. I think it was from his college days. Rumor has it that he was going pro but hurt his knee and had to quit.

I went to his office not knowing what to expect. He asked me to sit. I just stood there for a second. Old memories of getting fired started playing through my head. "Come on Sam, sit. I'm not going to bite you," he said. I sat reluctantly and left the door open in case I had to get out quickly.

Then he started talking. "Sam, I've been keeping a close eye on you since you arrived." Oh no, here we go. I was ready to go pack my things and leave. Then he went on. "I have to tell you that you are one of the best workers I have ever had here at the mission."

Wow, I didn't expect that. I expected to get yelled at for something. I'm not sure why. I hadn't done anything wrong. I did work hard. I didn't complain. For some reason, I reverted to the Sam of old who was always looking over his back to cover his tracks. I was thinking like the Sam who didn't work hard and did complain. It takes a long time to change old habits.

"Thanks" was all I could come up with.

He went on. "Here's the deal, Sam. I need a full-time employee. I have a permanent position that I need to fill, and I think you're the man for the job. What do you think?"

What did I think? I had a million things going through my mind. I'll be honest with you. All of a sudden I was scared. Fear came over me and I had to get out of there as soon as I could.

I told him that I would think about it and get back with him soon. Then I high-tailed it out of there as if my chair was on fire. I walked down the street and caught the trolley down to the wharf. I had been spending a lot of thinking time down there over the past month and found that it brought me a sense of calm.

It was the Fourth of July and it was busy there. People were coming from all over the city to see the fireworks display over the bay. It made me think of you. I remember back when you were a little girl maybe about 5 or 6. We were still living in Forest Lake. Every year they would have this huge firework display on the water downtown. We would go every year that we lived there. I can remember sitting in the park right on the water with our blanket spread on the grass. As it got darker the anticipation for the show would build. Kids would set off fire-crackers and bottle rockets in the streets. Every time one of them would go off you would jump and hide your head on my chest.

When it was totally dark and the show was just about to start, you wanted to go home. You were afraid of the noise and smoke and people. I held you tight and told you that everything was going to be OK. But you wouldn't have it. You wanted to go home right then. You didn't like what was going on, and you didn't want to see the pretty fireworks.

Then out of nowhere, the first big rocket would shoot up into the air. You held your breath and then poof—a beautiful red and white display of lights filled the sky. You were mesmerized. Then the next one went off and this time blue lights exploded overhead. You would yell out the colors. All of a sudden, you weren't afraid anymore.

When the show was over, you were disappointed and didn't want to go home. Your mother and I would just laugh. Those were good times.

So there I was, an old man sitting at the wharf waiting for the fireworks to start and I was scared out of my wits, wanting to run away. For some reason, my discussion with Brother Ron brought a sense of fear to me that I had not felt in a long time. I didn't know what to think of it. Considering the situation, what did I have to fear? I was clean and sober, working hard, and getting recognized for it. But I was afraid.

I remember Jason talking about this type of thing in one of our group sessions in Seattle. He told us that there were many types of fears in life—fear of failure, fear of the unknown, and the strangest one to me, fear of success. You wouldn't think people would be afraid of that. You would think that people want to succeed and that they would run toward the opportunities to succeed. He told us that many times the opposite is true.

For some, success is a huge fear because when they do something that brings a certain amount of success, then they will be expected to perform at that level again or better. Many people are afraid that they can't do it again or better, so they sabotage themselves and do things that will only allow them to have a limited amount of success.

All of a sudden, I saw a pattern in my life. I had many jobs that I was good at, and when I was a young man working at the mill I had worked my way up to a management position. Then I lost my family and felt like a complete failure. No amount of business success could bring any of that back. I felt no matter what I did in business or life, I was already a failure.

I had several jobs in the past that were going well. I would get recognized for my work and get promoted. That was a death sentence for me and whoever I was working for at the time. As soon as I started moving up, something in me said I was going to screw it up eventually so I might as well quit. Sure enough, I would start to mess up, come in late or not finish assignments. I mean, what did it matter? I was going to get fired anyhow. Might as well get it over with.

When Brother Ron offered me the full-time position, all of those feelings came back to me. I didn't know what to do. That night I watched the fireworks and thought of you and the fears in my life.

The next morning I called Jason to see what he thought about Brother Ron's job offer. He listened as I told him my fear of success story. He said what I was dealing with was very common and that people deal with fears differently. All I had to do was identify where this fear was coming from, and I could renew my mind in this area of my life.

He explained that many times fears are based on a belief system that we all build based on our experiences in life. Part of this system is based on what our parents taught us as children, what we learned at school, church, from our friends, but most of all from our life experiences.

"What is it that made you afraid of success, Sam," he asked.

I thought about it for a while, but didn't have an answer. He said that most people who are afraid of success had something happen in their past that made them think they didn't deserve to succeed. Something in their belief system that tells them "You're not good enough," or "You don't deserve it." This belief system breeds fear and causes confusion.

Jason said that there is a Scripture that says that God did not give us a spirit of fear, but one of power, love, and a sound mind. If we are afraid of something, then we know this is not from God.

"So Sam, the question here is, what do you believe about yourself and success? Do you think that you deserve to be a success?" Jason asked me.

I couldn't answer him. The phone was silent.

"Sam, are you there?"

"Yes, yes I'm here. I don't know how to answer that question. Can I think about it?"

"Take all the time you need, you have my number."

I hung up and sat staring at the phone for a good long time.

The truth is, Kathleen, somewhere way deep down inside me, I don't believe I should be successful. How can I be? I left my little girl on Christmas Eve. I'm a failure. At least that's what I believed up to that point. I knew I needed to change my thinking. But how?

When I went to bed that night, Jason's words kept running through my mind. What was my belief system? Could I be a success? Did I deserve to be a success? Could I renew my mind? For the first time on my own, I knelt down by the side of my bed and I prayed. I prayed to God and asked Him to help me renew my mind. I asked Him to show me what my belief system was and to show me what it *should* be. Then I went to bed.

When I woke up the next morning, I had a new outlook on life. I had a sense of hope like I had not experienced before. I knew if I could step up and face my fears—I could make it to the finale.

I went to Brother Ron's office and asked if I could talk with him. I told him of the fear that came to me when he offered me the job. I told him about my conversations with Jason and how I had actually prayed about this situation. He listened and smiled. Then I told him that I wanted the job just to prove to myself that I could do it and not screw it up. As soon as I said, "I'll take the job," something in me changed. There was no fear. I actually felt peace. Even more, I was excited!

For the first time in a long time I did not let my fear make my decisions or dictate my life. I stood up to it; and because of that, I broke the chains of the past that held me down from moving on in my life. I was able to renew my mind in this area and rewrite my belief system. I now believe that it is OK for me to succeed. It is OK for me to do well. The difference now is that it is not about me succeeding to prove anything to anyone. It is about me living to my fullest potential. Living a fearless life.

Kathleen, my next gift to you is the *Gift of Living a Fearless Life.*

I hope that any fears in your past would not dictate your future—that your belief system would be written so that you live your dream free from worry or fear. My desire is that you do not have a spirit of fear, but one of power, love, and a sound mind.

Live a fearless life.

# *Restored*

## *August 31, Purpose*

### *San Francisco, California*

It has been awhile since my last post. I have been very busy working with Brother Ron for about a month and a half, and I have to tell you that it has been one of the most rewarding times in my life. He is an amazing man who has a heart the size of Texas. I watch him and see how he deals with the daily routine and how he treats people. He has to face so many situations each day that would make me want to spit, but he handles them with a grace like I have never seen.

In several instances, he was dealing with guys who had lied or not followed through with what they said they would do and it put him in a bad place. He didn't get upset and yell, he just asked questions and dealt with the person calmly and in complete control.

How he did it was way beyond me. I would have grabbed those guys by the throat and threw them out the door. But he reminded me that we all have issues that we need to deal with and the grace that he was showing them at that time was designed to help them grow. I guess he was right.

One day we were working in the recreation area, getting it ready for a fund-raising event that was the next day. I was setting chairs, and he was working on the computer and the projector. I was wondering why this man had dedicated his life to what he was doing. With all the things he could do, why pick this? So I had to ask him.

I went over to him and sat by him as he worked on his computer.

"Brother Ron…" I said.

"Sam, you can just call me Ron. We're friends," he said smiling as he typed on the keyboard.

"Well, OK then, Ron. Why are you doing what you do?"

He looked up from the computer screen and gave me a quizzical look. "What do you mean, Sam?"

"I mean with all the talents and abilities you have, why do you put up with all the crap that these men give you? I know you can't be making a lot of money doing this."

He just smiled and nodded his head.

"Why work for little money and high stress?" I asked.

Brother Ron looked around the room and then looked back at me. "Sam, what do you see here?"

"What do you mean?" I asked.

"Look around you, what is it that you see?"

I looked around the room for a moment. We were sitting in the middle of a gymnasium.

I think at one time this building was an old YMCA or something. It had hardwood floors with a domed roof. Basketball hoops on each end with worn wooden pull-out bleachers. I looked back at him and said, "I see a gym."

"Yes, you're right," he said. "But what is this gym?"

"A place for people to play basketball."

He smiled at my answer and then leaned back in his chair. "You're right again. To one person this is an old building that we use to exercise. But to me it is much more than that. To me it is a reward. It's a reward for the work I am doing. It's also a tool, a tool to change the lives of all the men who come into this building. You have to understand, Sam, when you dedicate your life to something, you are not working for a paycheck or a pension. You are working for the reward. If you work for money, you will never be satisfied. It really is a mind shift. You can do a work and hope it will fulfill all of your needs, but if you are working for a wage then that is all you will ever get. You need to find a work that has a purpose.

"You can work your whole life away and make all kinds of money, but without purpose, you will never be satisfied. God made us to be creatures of purpose. He has put in us the inherent ability to create and to work with purpose. When we are dedicated to something that is bigger than us, then we never work for a paycheck. We earn a reward. Nothing can give you more satisfaction than receiving a reward versus being paid."

Then he stopped talking and looked me in the eye. Kathleen, I really didn't know what to say. Before I left you and your mom, I had measured my success by how much money I had made and I was constantly full of stress. But here I was looking at a man who was the most peaceful, content person I had ever met. And he was telling me that money has nothing to do with happiness. This has been a recurring theme with all of the "successful" people I've met.

After a moment of piercing my soul with his eyes, he said, "You see Sam, I used to do the whole climb the corporate ladder thing, but it seemed to me the more 'successful' I became, the less happy I was. I worked to build a small empire for myself so I would look 'valuable' to anyone who saw me. They'd see I was important. In the end, I realized that it was all hollow. Now don't get me wrong. There are a lot of good men and women in the corporate world who have their priorities right."

That made me think of Jim.

"It was just that for me, I had to get out of that atmosphere and get into one that promoted more of a giving lifestyle," he said.

"So you started the mission?" I asked.

"No, I started to volunteer here. You know, the typical times of the year—Thanksgiving and Christmas. But then the manager of the mission asked me if I could help out more often. For some reason it intrigued me, so I started helping out once a month on Saturdays.

"Over the years I volunteered more and more until one day, just like you, Jason came into town and offered me a full-time job. I didn't know what to think. That would mean letting go of the corporate job I held that I hated, but I thought it was what I needed to do to feel fulfilled. I was not married, so leaving my job wouldn't affect anyone but me. I had to get over the feeling, though, that I would be stepping down in the ranks of life if I took the job at the mission. After much thought and prayer, I took the job. That was ten years ago."

That was an amazing story. I just had one more question for him. "Are you glad you did it?" I could tell by the look on his face that this was not the first time he had been asked that question.

I'll be honest with you, at first it was not easy. I questioned myself all the time. I was actually about to quit after the third month. But then something happened.

"I'll never forget it. It was about nine on a Thursday night. I was in my office working on the budget to present to the board when I heard a noise downstairs at the front door. I knew I was the only one in the building, so I went down to the front door to see who was there. When I opened the door, I didn't see anyone and was about to close the door when I heard a noise. I saw some movement a few yards away and went to see what it was. Just behind the dumpster there was a body lying in the shadows. He looked as though he had been badly beaten. I took him inside and called the ambulance. The EMTs came and took him to the hospital.

"I went to the hospital to follow up on him. I found out his name was Joseph. I visited him over the next few weeks and we got to know each other. He was pretty beat up. He had a couple of broken ribs and bruises on his face. He wasn't sure what happened. All he knew was that he was walking alongside the road, and then he was hit. When he regained consciousness, he remembered our mission so he came here for help.

"As he recovered, we spent a lot of time together. The day came for his discharge, and I invited him to stay at the mission until he could get back on his feet. He came and took part in our 12-step classes—I like to call them opportunity classes. He took all of the classes to heart and started making changes in his life. He got cleaned up, drug free, and got a job at the local fast food joint. He worked hard and showed himself worthy of promotion. The manager noticed and started promoting him. Today he is the district manager of that chain and loving every minute of his life. He met a nice lady at the restaurant and after two years of 'courting,' they got married. I'm sure you've seen him. He comes in here a couple times a month to help out."

"Oh yeah, Joey. I've seen him. He's a real nice guy. He came from here? I can't believe that. He seems so put together. So because of Joe you're glad you did it?" I asked.

"No, Sam. Because I had found a purpose for my life I was glad I did it. The day that I made my life bigger than myself was the day that I found purpose. I took the job because I was asked to. I was not happy with my present job so what could it hurt? I found my life the day I realized that I had a purpose in this life and that was to help other people. The day we can come to the realization that life is not about us, it is about others is the day we can truly be free. Helping Joseph showed me that there was more to life than making money and owning things. Helping him showed me that true satisfaction comes from helping others achieve their goals. There is a satisfaction in doing this that no amount of money can match.

"You have to understand, I still need money to live. We all do. But now I am rewarded for the work that I have dedicated my life to. You have heard it said, 'If you love what you do, you will never work a day in your life'? Well, I'm here to tell you that it's true. If you dedicate yourself to something bigger than yourself, you will find your purpose in life, and you will never work another day in your life."

At that he smiled and breathed a heavy, satisfying breath. I didn't know what to say other than, "Amen." We both laughed for a moment and then I thanked him for sharing his story with me—it meant a lot.

Kathleen, my next gift to you is the *Gift of Purpose.* It is my desire that you find something bigger than yourself that defines your purpose in life. I hope that you never have to work a day in your life because you are doing what you love, and that you find satisfaction that money can't buy. True peace and satisfaction in life come only from having a sense of purpose. It is my wish for you to have a purpose in life and follow your dreams to that end.

Kathleen, you have a purpose.

# September 2, Choice

## San Francisco, California

For the past few days, I have been working with Brother Ron on our fund-raising banquet. We are expecting about 250 people. Hopefully, this event will raise the money needed for the building improvements.

I was thinking about some of the things Brother Ron was saying to me the other day. Mostly about having a purpose in life. I can't say that I ever had that feeling of purpose in the past. I guess I could say that my only purpose was just to survive, but that's really no purpose, just an existence. We talked a little more today and he told me that everything we do is by choice, whether we know it or not. Staying somewhere or leaving is a choice. Being happy or sad is a choice. Loving and hating are both choices. Taking advantage of an opportunity or coming up with an excuse—choice.

He said that one of the biggest lies that people live is that they believe they are stuck where they are and that there is no getting out of it. They think they have to play with the cards that they were dealt. He said that was a huge lie that will trap you in a life that you don't want. Most people deal with this type of lie in their jobs. They are in a job that they don't like, but stay there because they don't know what else they can do. The truth is, they are not willing to step out beyond the comfort zone they created to see other possibilities.

The strange fact is that many people stay in a bad situation or bad job because it is all they know. Many times people who grow up in an abusive relationship will enter another one when they are older. Not because they want to be abused, but because it's all they know. They are familiar with it and so they return to it.

Brother Ron told me a story of a horse rancher who had some prized horses in his barn. One night there was a fire in the barn. He risked his life to go into the burning barn to get the horses out. One by one he opened stalls and chased the horses out of the barn into the pasture. The fire was consuming the barn and he narrowly escaped with his life. Moments after he ran out, he saw something he never expected. The horses were completely freaked out by the fire and they were running around behind the barn. Then one of them ran back into the barn. Then another and another until they were all back in the barn. Why did they do that? Why would they run right back into danger when they were safe?

To the horses, the stall was a safe place. When there was bad weather, the rancher would put the horses in their stalls to protect them.

Now, even though there was danger in the barn, they ran into their stalls to be safe because it was the only thing they knew. Unfortunately, they all died.

He told me this story to drive the point home. Some people, just like the horses, run back to what they know even if it is the very thing causing them harm. Even when things are going good in their lives, they will leave that and return to their comfort zone for a false sense of safety. Sadly, this becomes a pattern in life until the person is willing to step out of their comfort zone, use a little faith, face their fears, and go to a new place.

In reality, I don't think all of this is really possible without knowing your Creator. He is the Source of strength and the Guide to those who are lost. Many people try to fill the emptiness in their lives with all types of things that only He can fill. I hope and pray that you have come to a saving knowledge of Christ, but many have not and they try to find their way through life without Him. I don't know how I would have gotten this far in my life without His guiding hand. But that's just me.

Up until a few months ago, I would have thought what Brother Ron was saying was gibberish. But now, after coming to know Christ in a personal way, I knew he was right. And I knew he was talking about me. We both knew that it was time for me to start seeing things differently and go to a place where I had not gone in the past.

"Sam," he said, "I have to apologize to you."

"To me? What on earth for?"

"Sam, when I offered you this job, I did it out of my needs, not yours. I needed someone with your skills to help me. Don't get me wrong, you have done a great job and you have become a good friend..."

Now I was confused. Was I getting fired? "Are you firing me?" I asked him.

He laughed out loud. "No, no but I am releasing you to go do what you need to do. Your job is here as long as you want it. I just want you to know that if you need to go, there would be no hard feelings."

I knew what he was talking about. I had told him about you and that I was on my way back to see you. Then I realized the significance of the horse story. I was once again hiding in my work and not facing the issues I needed to in my life. Every day that I worked with Ron was a day that I was not coming back to see you. Even though the work was good, and I was doing great things helping others, it was still a burning barn to me.

Once again, I was hiding from what I should be doing with my family. The crazy part is that anyone looking at me and what I am doing would say that I am doing good things. I am making a difference in others' lives and I am gainfully employed. Those are all good things. The only problem is that I should be going to see you.

I had all of these thoughts going through my head as Ron and I stood looking at each other.

Then he broke the silence, "That's all I needed to say, Sam. I hope you understand what I am saying."

"Yes, I think I do," I said. Then he leaned over and hugged me. This was the first time, and I didn't know how to react. I gave him a slight hug and a pat on the back. Then he walked away.

I felt as though he had just led me out of the stall and now I was standing outside of the barn looking in. Now it was up to me. I knew what I needed to do. To be honest, it scares me. There are so many unknowns in going to see you. What if you hate me? What if you tell me you don't want to see me? I don't know if I can face that kind of rejection. That is what has stopped me so many times over the years. Being rejected is my biggest fear in life. I have worked hard to gain the approval of those around me. When I get it, I feel safe for a while but then, just like the barn, the sense of approval is what would burn me. I was trying to gain the approval from others that I needed from you.

Now I am faced with the same decision that I have been running away from ever since that night that I left you. I need to find you and ask you to forgive me. This is the hardest thing that I have ever had to do in my life. Not because I don't want to ask you to forgive me, but because I am afraid that you won't.

This morning I went to Ron and I gave him my resignation. He was not surprised. In fact, he was happy.

"I know this is what you need to do," he said. "Go out into the pasture. Go out into the unknown and the uncertain and go after that one thing that will set you free from you past. Remember that you are not going alone. Remember that you have your Creator going with you and He will help you through this transition. You only have to be willing to take the first steps. He will not force you into any situation. He will walk alongside you and give you guidance.

There is a Scripture in the Old Testament that says God has set before us the choice of life and death. Then it goes on to say He tells us to choose life. When I picture this in my mind I see a father talking with his child. They had walked way up on a mountain and they could see the whole world. They could see all of the good in the world and all of the bad. Then the father says, 'Here is the whole world set before you. You can do and be whatever you want. You can have life or you can have death. The choice is yours.' After a moment of taking it all in, the father looks the child straight in the eyes and says, 'I suggest you choose life.'

"He is not saying that choosing life will be the easy choice. In most cases it is the harder choice. The choices we make lead to more choices of the same. The more life we choose, the more life we will get so that we can choose more life. The same is true with death. The more we make those choices, the more we will have the effects of death in our lives.

"Making the right choice is not always the easy thing to do. We have to look beyond ourselves and see how our decisions affect those around us. You have to ask yourself, 'Am I willing to put the needs of others above my own? Will this bring more life to me? Am I willing to sacrifice my wants for those of my family?' Knowing the answers to these questions will bring life.

"Sam, for me the more I live to help others, the more I truly find a peace in life. The more I choose life, the more real living I have to live.

"I know this may sound like a puzzle, but it is one puzzle that is worth figuring out. Go after it, Sam. Go after life. Be willing to put your doubts and fears down and make the tough choice to go after your daughter. Choose her over your own comfort. Like I said, going to face her and ask her to forgive you will not be the easy thing to do. But it will be the thing that brings healing to her and to you. This brings life to both of you."

He didn't have to say anything more. I had already made up my mind to leave, but it was nice of him to confirm that I was making the right choice. So Kathleen, I am leaving to find you. I have to go to San Diego to clear up some loose ends and then I will be on my way to see you. I hope to make it there by Christmas. I have a present that I want to give to you.

The next gift I give you is the *Gift of Choice*. I hope you have a clear understanding of what the right choice is when you are faced with choices in your life. It is my prayer that you always choose life.

Kathleen—make choices, don't allow others or situations to choose for you.

# Restored

## October 10

### San Diego, California

I left San Francisco right after my last letter to you. I am in San Diego. Part of my journey back to you is getting all of my affairs in order. I spent many years in San Diego when I was younger and I had a relationship with a woman that lasted for several years. Like most of my other relationships, this one did not end well. I feel that I need to make amends with her before I come to see you.

Unfortunately, I was not able to find her, which makes this whole trip very difficult for me. On top of that, I have gotten sick again. I have been battling this for a while now. I am stuck in the hospital. My doctor says I am in the final stages of emphysema. It just hit me hard the last few weeks, until I had such a hard time breathing I had to go into the hospital. They are telling me that I will be in here for a while. I hope this is not true.

I'm not sure what to think. I really believe that I need to see you. I have never believed something so strongly in my life before. But it seems as if it is not meant to be. I'm sorry to sound so negative, but I am not sure what to think right now. I'll write more later when I know more.

# Restored

## November 1

### San Diego, California

I was really hoping the new month would bring new news. I am still in the hospital. They are giving me regular treatments. It seems like I am getting better, but all they say to me is, "We will have to wait and see." I really want to get to you before Christmas. I pray every day and ask the Lord to let me see you before I die.

The journey that I have taken over the past year has been life-transforming. I can't understand why He would bring me this far and not let me see this all the way to the end. I'm sure this is what He wanted me to do.

I'll write more later. It's time for a treatment.

# Restored

## December 15

### San Diego, California

It has been over a month since my last letter to you. I fear that the end is near. I know that I must see you. I tried calling the number I had found for you, but the message said the number was disconnected. I could not find another listing for you in Tulsa. Now I'm not sure if you still live in Tulsa. I have set up a meeting with a lawyer on Friday to have him help me find you and get in touch with you. I don't want to die without having talked with you, Katy. It is important that I ask for your forgiveness. I have to go now. Even writing this little bit has made me very tired.

# Restored

## December 21, New Life

### Tulsa, Oklahoma

$\mathcal{J}$'m not sure how to start this letter. I'm not really sure what has happened. I guess I'll just start from what I remember.

I was in San Diego in the hospital. I had met with my lawyer about getting in contact with you. He was going to work on it. I remember being so weak that I could hardly lift my hand to change the channel on the television. I tried to write more to you, but even that was painful.

Then one morning I awoke and everything seemed different. I was lying in my bed, and I had an incredible sense of peace all over me, a peace that I have never experienced before. I think it was Monday morning. The doctors and nurses came into the room in a rush and started pushing buttons on the machines and sticking needles in me. I couldn't feel a thing— only an overwhelming sense of peace. Then I went to sleep.

Moments later, it seemed as if I was flying. I was above my body watching them work on me. They used the paddles on me. Every time they hit the button, my body lurched. I could see my face. It was pale and expressionless. I watched this for what seemed like an hour but I know it was just a few moments. Then they stopped. They all left my room. I could tell by their reactions that this was a routine event to them. I started to go higher and the room got smaller and smaller until I was in total blackness. Then I saw a light way off in the distance, and I could hear the sound of a car coming toward me.

All of a sudden I was standing in the middle of the road as a car slid to a stop right in front of me. I looked up and there you were looking through your windshield right at me. I thought I was dreaming. But I knew it wasn't a dream because I could feel the air on my face. I felt strong and energized. You said you were sorry, and then I walked to the side of the road. I watched as you drove away. I really didn't know what to do.

What was going on? Was I dead? Was I a ghost? Or maybe an angel? I'm not sure. All I knew was that I had a chance to make things right, and I was going to take full advantage of that opportunity. I watched you park your car and go into a store. You seemed in a hurry, so I figured I would wait for you to come out. Then I would talk to you. After about a half hour, you came out of the store and walked toward your car. Again you seemed to be very much in a hurry.

As you were getting into your car, I started walking over to you. Out of the dark a couple of punks appeared, riding their skateboards toward you. I was proud at how you handled them. Their threats didn't seem to faze you one bit. But without thinking, I jumped in to help you, and the kid blind-sided me with his skate-board, and I went down. So much for me trying to rescue you.

When I awoke, you were standing over me. You looked like an angel. You didn't recognize me, of course—it had been so long since you watched me walk away that Christmas Eve. I was at a loss for words. I mean, there you were after almost three decades of wondering about the woman you had become. What you looked like, sounded like, even smelled like. You were so beautiful and so in control. I wanted to reach out and hold you. I wanted to tell you I was sorry. I wanted to be healed. I wanted you to be healed.

We talked about nothing for a couple of awkward moments, and then you left. What was I doing? I let you go. I didn't know what to do next, so I went back to the bus shelter. I started praying and asking God to bring you back to me. I was about ready to cry when I heard your car pull up. There you were again. For a moment you looked like that little 10-year-old girl staring at me through the window. Again I was at a loss for words.

You offered me a ride. Those were the most beautiful words I had ever heard. I knew the bus station would be closed, but I couldn't be so forward as to ask to stay with you. I knew it would have to be your idea. When we got to the bus station and you realized that it was closed, you invited me to stay at your home for the night because you knew I didn't have anywhere else to stay. I was elated. Those words were like breath to me. I could hardly contain myself, but I knew I couldn't let it show. I knew I had to approach this whole situation slowly, or I would scare you away.

When you pulled into your driveway, I saw your little girl, Lucy, sleeping on the couch. I was so happy that you had a family. This meant I was a grandpa. Wow. But it wasn't true. It seemed as though you didn't even like this little girl. How could you not—she was a sleeping angel. She reminded me so much of you when you were a little girl.

In the morning we were hit with a beautiful snowstorm. It was as if Heaven were smiling on me. This would give me some more time with you. You seemed so out of sorts. Not the way I had imagined you. Things were not going the way you had planned, and I could see it was hard for you to handle not being in control of the situation.

Right now you are in the other room with Lucy, looking for a game for her. I want so much to tell you who I am but I have this strange sense of peace telling me that I need to wait. Time seems to be the key in this situation. I will wait and see what happens next.

Oh my...Lucy is here, and I must play a game with her. More later.

_Restored_

# December 22, Forgiveness

## Tulsa, Oklahoma

It's just past midnight. I am sitting in the living room by the fireplace. You have just gone to bed. This has to be one of the most difficult nights of my life. Your interaction with Lucy was painful to watch. Lucy is so much like you. The two of you have faced a very painful experience in your lives that have handicapped you both emotionally. In you I can see the effects of carrying this pain around with you for the past 25 years. In her I can see what you must have been like while I was gone.

Seeing this opens up old wounds. Why am I here? Is this a punishment for me? Reliving this pain is almost more than I can bear. Looking into your eyes and listening to you describe what it was like for you when I left has ripped my heart out. How will you ever be able to forgive me?

When I was sharing my story with you, I was hoping that in some small way you would tell me it was OK, that you wouldn't hate someone like me. I was looking for any glimmer of forgiveness from you. After listening to you talk, I know that is not the case. I'm not sure if that will ever be the case.

I wanted to tell you who I was but I know this is still not the time. I wish I knew for certain when the time will be right. I am hoping that through our meeting you will be able to forgive me, and most of all you will be able to forgive your mother.

I could tell by the way you spoke of your mother that you blamed her for all of your pain. In reality, I am the author of the pain you have experienced. I have learned that forgiveness is the key to peace.

In my travels over the past 25-some years, I have seen a lot of people in a lot of pain. The pain they carry becomes heavy baggage that only holds them back from who they can be and should be in life. The hardest thing to understand about unforgiveness is that it is the highest form of selfishness. Those who carry all the hurts of their past do so because, in a strange way, they feel justified by this pain. They feel that they deserve to be mad or upset with whoever hurt them.

Carrying pain around builds a foundation of selfishness and self-centeredness. The pain justifies how they feel and they think punishes those who have caused them pain. But really, all this does is hurt the person who is carrying the unforgiveness. Many times the people who have caused the pain don't even know that they have done so. They go on with their lives and the unforgiving person is the one who continues in pain because she hasn't let go of the baggage.

In your case, I can see the pain in your life. I see this very controlled life that you have built for yourself. It seems you think that if you can control your surroundings, you will have peace. I have seen this countless times in our sessions at the mission. Men would come into the classes keeping others around them at arm's length, always trying to control their lives and every situation so they won't get hurt. They believe that if they don't let people in, then they won't get hurt.

Kathleen, I see the same thing with you. Tonight when you had your conversation with Lucy, she hit you with a bit of truth that was hard for you to face. Your reaction was to lash out at her—to control the situation and stop the questions. This shut her down. The sad fact is that you hurt the little girl and drove another wedge between the two of you.

After she stormed out of the room, you opened up for the first time. I finally felt as if the true Kathleen was showing through, if only for a few minutes. It seemed to me that it was the first time you were able to share the pain that you have been carrying with you for the past 25 years. The good news is that just being able to talk about it is the first step to forgiveness. You may not understand this, but you sharing your story with me, even just for a few minutes, will start the healing process.

Those who are not willing to forgive create a prison around themselves that locks up their emotions and feelings from the rest of the world—like being locked up in solitary confinement. People are not meant to be alone. People were created to create. When you isolate yourself from other people, you lock out this creative part of your life and handicap yourself in emotional and spiritual growth.

Jason shared with me one time that when a person has a tragic event in their lives, they will many times not mature emotionally beyond the point of that event until they come to terms with the person or persons in the event. This is true; I have seen it many times. People who have a tragic event when they are young still think and react as if they were still that child. The key to moving beyond is being able to look beyond ourselves and forgive. People must be willing to let go of the chains that bind them concerning an individual or many individuals. The chains of unforgiveness hold us back from growing. The worst part is that they hold us back from loving.

Without forgiveness, we will carry the pains and hurts of our past with us and they weigh us down to the point that we will never be able to fulfill our true destiny in life. We will always make decisions with a veil of pain in front of us. We try to self-preserve so we won't get hurt again. Our decisions are tainted and always point back to self-preservation. These type of decisions lead to death.

Every day you are faced with opportunities to go toward life or death. Forgiveness leads you toward life and unforgiveness leads toward death. Selfishness leads toward death and self-lessness leads toward life. Every day you have the opportunity to choose. Remember, always choose life. The first step to choosing life is to forgive.

Kathleen, this is my last letter to you. I feel my time will be coming to an end soon. I am not sure when I will leave, or how it will happen. All I know is I will be leaving you soon. I can feel it in my bones. I do not want to go, but I know my time here is short.

One thing that is most important for me to leave with you is that you forgive and receive forgiveness. Don't let the pain of the past define who you are today, or who you could be. Release those who you have held for all these years. You will never know true peace in your life until you forgive and are forgiven. Forgiveness is the key to living. You will not truly live your life to the fullest carrying the baggage of the past. Let go of the past. Choose to forgive. Say it out loud. I choose to forgive. It will set you free.

Kathleen, the last gift I give to you is the *Gift of Forgiveness*. Live to forgive. Live a life of true peace.

# Epilogue

Sam was only able to be with Kathleen for one more day. His time with her had come to an end. What she didn't know and what she would soon find out is that his personal effects had been sent to her on the day she met him. They were in a box sitting on her front doorstep the entire time Sam was with her. For some reason nobody noticed.

She had made arrangements to have dinner with Sam, Andrew, her boyfriend, and Lucy, Andrew's little girl. The past few days with Sam had been healing to her. She was able to face the pain of her past and was willing to let go and move on. This brought her a new sense of peace in her life in a way she had never experienced before.

On the last day they were together, Kathleen had to pick up Andrew at the airport and put in a full day at the restaurant. When she returned home to pick Sam up for dinner he was gone. Once again she felt abandoned and fell back into the gloomy world of self-doubt. Then she found the package. In that package were several gifts for her including this journal, all of which answered many questions she had about her life.

What she didn't know is that she would see him one last time.

*A Christmas Snow.*

# Restored

## Applying the Truths of Sam's Letters to Your Life

The first half of Sam's life was full of selfish ambition—his last half was led by fear of success and rejection. In the end, the journey he made to find his daughter was filled with truths that led him to fulfillment and to recognizing the gifts he had to leave her.

Many people go through life thinking that obtaining material possessions will bring peace and happiness, but in the end, they realize that it was all for nothing. They sacrificed everything to be labeled a "success," only to find themselves alone and lonely. Many use their family as an excuse to build their empire, "I work hard so you have a nice house and nice things." They think that providing their family with things shows them love. In reality, their spouse and children would rather have the person spend quality time with them than have all of the material stuff.

The largest house on the block will never replace time spent together with those who love you. An expensive car can't replace a walk with your spouse, children, parent, or a friend on a nice evening. Expensive trips will never replace making snow angels in the snow.

Things are nice to have, but they will never replace time with loved ones. Unfortunately for Sam, he did not realize this until the end of his life. At the end, all he wanted was time—time with his daughter and time to find forgiveness.

Right now you have the opportunity to apply the life lessons that Sam had the opportunity to learn the last year of his life. All of these lessons lead you toward a life full of peace, joy, and fulfillment. Applying even a few of them will change your life for the better.

## *The Gift of Faith*

Everyone has faith. The question is—what do you have faith in? Many have faith in themselves. Some have faith in the great cosmos that good things will happen because, "I am a good person." Others have faith in the stock market or their education or even their horoscope.

It is my belief that there is a Creator we can see and know. This Creator created you to have a relationship with Him. He tells you in the Bible that if you seek Him, you will find Him (see Matt. 7:7). Part of your being is made to have a relationship with the Creator, and many times you fill it with other things—we all do.

You will continue to search for this relationship in your life until it is filled. You are a spiritual being at your core and you will look for a spiritual relationship until you fill it with the One who created you.

Sam was unable to seek healing from those he hurt until he himself was made whole spiritually. He did this by choosing to have a relationship with his Creator. This relationship comes by having faith in your Creator and living your life through Him. If you don't have a relationship with your Creator, my first suggestion is to read the Book of John in the Bible. There are many Christian books that can help you seek Him out.

Just remember that if you look for him you will find him. If you knock the door will be opened. It takes some work on your part, but the reward is worth the effort.

## The Gift of Courage

Like other emotions that we deal with, fear can be a controlling emotion. People can actually experience physical effects from fear. Think about what it was like the first time you had to do something that you were afraid of doing. There can be physical reactions to fear such as shaking, sweating, crying, getting a headache or stomach ache, and even vomiting. Many people live their lives without the courage to face their fears. They make many decisions based on trying to be safe. Fear can lock you up and limit who you can be and who you should be. (See First John 4:18.)

If you want to live your life to its fullest, you need to have the courage to face your fears. How do you do that? Do something that you are afraid of. Find something that you know you need to do that scares you, and go do it. This may be something big, or it may be something small. Either way, go do it.

You will find that after you start doing things that you were afraid to do in the past, you will experience life in a new way. Letting go of fears is one of the most liberating experiences you will ever have. Why is having courage such a big deal? Because a life full of fear is a lie. When you have fears that hold you back, then what you believe about situations and circumstances are lies. The truth is, you can do anything or be anyone you want to be. All you have to do is retrain your mind so that you can believe it and be willing to face the fear and overcome it.

Trust me. This will not be easy. The truth is, anything that comes easy in life is usually not worth having. It is the things that we work for and really apply ourselves to that are filled with true riches. Look inside your self and muster up that childlike courage that is willing to believe there is nothing you can't do. Go after it. Do it today. Don't let any person, thing, or fear hold you back. If you go after it, you will make it happen. Face your fears and do that thing that you really want to do. Find the courage to face your fears and be the person you really want to be and should be.

## The Gift of a Legacy

There are three stages that we go through in life. The first 25 years are called the entitlement stage. This is when you are young and think that people owe you. It is a very selfish stage in life that some never grow out of. The second stage is the status stage. This is the stage where you try to establish yourself as a label. For example; My name is Fred and I am an engineer. Your status defines your level in life and your identity is built on that label. This too can be a selfish stage in life if it is not associated with a purpose. The third stage in life is the most important. It is the legacy stage. This is when you realize the important things in life are associated with other people. You are more concerned with what you will be leaving behind rather than what you can get while you are here.

A person who will leave a legacy has a future-thinking mind-set. People who think of the future and what they will leave behind are not selfish. These people understand what is truly important in life. They understand the value of the people around them. They understand that in this life we affect all those around us.

What will you leave behind when you are no longer on this planet? What will others say about you after you are gone? How will your days spent on this earth be remembered by others? The fact is, your life breaks down to nothing more than memories. When you die, people will not keep many, if any, of your physical effects. When your body is put into the ground, there will be nothing for others to hang on to except their memories of you.

Having a legacy mind-set helps you build a life worth remembering. When you make decisions with the mind-set of leaving a legacy, you will see things a little differently. You won't be moved so much by the temporal, but more by the eternal. You will think of what you are doing today and what will happen after you are gone. You will start to build a foundation on which your life will be remembered. You will build a life that will have a lasting effect ages after you've breathed your last.

It makes me think of the Founders of the United States of America. They were willing to give all they had so that those who would live after them would reap the benefits of their decisions. Many of those who signed the Declaration of Independence died with few material possessions. Many of the revolutionaries were killed for their acts, but they knew their purpose was much greater than their individual lives. They were willing to give it all so generations after them would live in a free country. They left a legacy by their actions. You and I are still reaping the benefits over 200 years later. (See Proverbs 13:22.)

When you have a legacy mind-set, your life is bigger than yourself. Many of the petty things that can distract you fall to the wayside. You start to see things differently and realize that everything you do will have a lasting effect, and then you will start to make your decisions based on that new mind-set. This mind-set also gives you a sense of purpose. With that sense of purpose guiding you, you will have a new perspective on life—a life full of endless possibilities. You will live a life that will leave a legacy.

# The Gift of Giving

Giving is the foundation to live a truly fulfilling and peaceful life. Much like the other gifts, giving directs the attention off you and toward others. What you do and the decisions you make have an effect on those around you. Good or bad, you are making a difference in the lives of people every day.

Giving is a mind-set that leads to a way of life. Giving causes you to see beyond your own life and your own needs and you start to see the needs of others. You may be afraid to give because you have a feeling of lack or that you won't have enough for yourself. But when you start to focus on those around you and ways that you can help them, you will find that everything you need will be provided. (See Luke 6:38.)

There are certain principles in our world that cannot be denied. One is the principle of sowing and reaping. You reap whatever it is that you sow in your life. If you sow seeds of life you will reap a harvest of life. If you sow seeds of selfishness, you will reap lack and will always be scrambling to get enough to survive. If you hang on to everything for yourself, and don't give, you will always lack in one way or another. The opposite is also true. If you give, you will find that you will be replenished and you will always have more than you need.

As is true with all of these gifts, it comes down to training your mind to see things differently. You must be willing to let go of your fear of lack and start where you are. Give what you can in all areas of life. This principle is not just about money—it is true in all aspects of life. Giving is a foundation that you can build your life on. The things that you want more of in your life—start giving those things to others. If you want more love, give more love. If you want more time, give time. If you want more friends, give friendship. Remember, this principle works in every area of life.

Let go of the feelings that you don't have enough. Give what you have, and you will see it come back to you. Learn to think like a giver. Let it become who you are not just what you do. You will find great reward in doing this.

## The Gift of Freedom

Freedom is a very strong word. People have died trying to obtain it, and many others have died defending it. You possess a freedom that cannot be granted or taken away. It is the ability to be free from your past. No matter what has happened to you, you have the ability to release it and move on. You do not have to be a prisoner to your past. In fact, you do not have to be a prisoner to your future. That's right, people can be prisoners to their future just as much as their past. The very thing that creates prisons is the same thing that can set you free from a life in prison—words. Words carry power. Words can lift you up and make you want to be a better person, or they can tear you down and make you want to kill yourself.

Prisons of the past are created by what someone may have said to you or about you when you were younger. It may be an event that left you scarred.

Prisons of the future are created today by the words that others may say about you, or by the words that you say about yourself. You can create new and thicker walls every day by repeating wrong or hurtful things that you have heard about yourself, and then you take them as truth and say them to yourself. If you believe it and say it, it will eventually happen. You are a creative being, and you create life and death with your words.

Freedom comes the very same way, by your words. You can break the prison of the past by believing and speaking what you want to *be* in your life, thus breaking any power that the past may have over you. You break the prisons of the future the very same way. When you hear someone say something to or about you that you don't want in your life, you can refute it and direct your thinking in the right direction at that very moment. (See John 8:32.)

This may sound like a magic trick, but quite the opposite is true. This is the foundation of who you are as a creative being. If you are made in the image of your Creator, then you are made to create. Whether you believe it or not, you do it every day. You create your life and where it is going every day. You do it first by your thoughts, and then with your words.

Your words can bring you freedom and no one or anything can stop it from happening. Learn the power of your words and let them set you free from any prison of your past *and* your future.

## The Gift of Family

This is one of the most valuable gifts we can ever have—the gift of family. There are many people in this world who have gone after many different types of success and lost the very thing that makes them successful. Family is the true definition of success. The relationship that you have with your spouse, children, parents, or extended family and friends, is the foundation of success. Many have chased after material success or fame only to lose the most important thing that truly defines success—family.

I would go so far as to say that if you do not have a success story with family members, then you will never truly be a success in anything else. If you are looking for something to define you as a success, look no farther than your own home. Until you are a success there, chasing after fortune and fame will leave you empty.

No doubt you have read many stories of people who have worked hard their whole lives to reach the pinnacle of fame and fortune only to despise the very thing that they thought would make them happy. I have read countless biographies of actors and musicians who had given everything to reach a high level of fame only to wish they hadn't sacrificed so much for fame that is fleeting. Many times they lost everything dear to them on the way to the top and when they finally got there, they were all alone. Then most turned to excessive drinking and drugs, because they sacrificed everything, had nothing when they reached their destination, and needed to fill the hole in their lives with something.

Family is the core of a person's life. We are made to have relationships with each other. None is more important than your family. Take the time to cultivate your family relationships. Make that the most important—and all the other things will fall nicely into place.

## The Gift of Creativity

As stated previously, it is important to understand that you are a creation who was created to create. It is something that you do every day. Every time you have a thought, you are creating. Sometimes you realize you are creating, but most times you probably don't. Your life right now is the sum total of the choices and decisions that you have made to this point. You have created your life and everything within it that you are experiencing.

You may ask, "How am I doing this?" The answer is very simple. You create first with your thoughts and then with your words. Your thoughts lead to words, which lead to action, which become reality. Nothing on this earth was ever invented that was not at first a thought. Everything you use on a daily basis was first a thought. Then that thought is shared with other people and it becomes a thought to them. Once this thought is discussed, it is then put down on paper and it becomes a tangible reality. From words and drawings, it is then manufactured into a physical reality.

Creating your life happens the same way. Your thoughts lead to your words and your words lead to reality. It's a very simple process after you understand it. An underlying factor makes this all possible—your subconscious.

Your subconscious is working 24/7/365. It never sleeps. It is always pondering and looking for ways to bring to life the things you are feeding it. Your subconscious is like a machine with only one purpose—to bring to life the information with which it is being presented.

Here is a good example. Think about the last car you have purchased. After you purchased it, did you notice cars just like yours on the street? Why is that? Did the manufacturer decide to make and sell more cars like yours just because you had purchased one? No. Now that you purchased the car, it is part of your life. Your subconscious is now more aware of it, which makes you more aware of the same car when you see it. Your subconscious will always find ways to bring the things that you are feeding it to reality.

Now here is the part that most people don't want to deal with. Since your subconscious is always at work on what you feed it, your life is a result of what you have been feeding it. If there are things in your life that you don't like, you have no one to blame but yourself. Bad habits, lifestyle, and work are all results of what you have thought on and dwelled on. The great thing about all of this is that if you don't like how your life is, you can change it. You have the ability to retrain your mind and bring to your life the things that you want.

Romans 12:2 says that you should not be conformed to this world and that you can be *transformed* by the renewing of your mind. You can change your world and life by renewing your thought process. When you change how you think, you change how you talk, and by doing that you change your life. Your life is a direct result of your thinking.

You are always creating. What you create is up to you.

## The Gift of Living a Fearless Life

As mentioned previously, at the base of most issues people deal with is fear. If you dig even deeper, you find selfishness. Some people will not move on with their lives because they are afraid. At one time or another in all of our lives, we will deal with some sort of fear. What we do with that fear determines what and who we will be in this life.

If it is more important for you to be approved by other people than yourself, then you will be crippled by your fear of approval. If you are not willing to look like a complete fool because you don't know what you're doing in any given situation, you will be limited by your fear of failure or fear of being humiliated. The list goes on and on. The fact is, you limit who you can be by allowing fear to dictate what you will do with your life.

One of the biggest lies that people deal with is believing that they are the only ones afraid of this or that. When you get hit with a fear, you think that you are the only one who has ever felt this way. But there is nothing new under the sun. The feelings that you feel are not new and they are not original. You do not feel anything different from what others have felt. There is one key difference between those who are successful and those who are not—the ones who are willing to face fear and conquer it are successful and will live life to the fullest.

How you look at fear and life really matters. Are you going to look at a situation and allow fear to dictate to you what you are capable of? Or are you going to make the decision to overcome it?

Those who don't do anything with their lives have all the good excuses, and to most people they sound legitimate. But all they are doing is hiding behind their fear. They have found a safe place that takes responsibility away from them. This is where the selfish part comes in. They are more concerned with preserving the life that they have than going out and becoming who they should be. The focus is on themselves and not on their family or friends.

What would happen if you were living the life you should be living? What if you worked a job that totally fulfilled you as a person? What would you be like if you felt completely fulfilled? Do you think this would affect those around you? Do you think you would be a positive influence on those you have contact with every day? I would venture to say yes.

Facing your fears and conquering them brings liberty, and with liberty comes peace. If you want to have peace in your life, go after your dreams. Face your fears and conquer them. Just by being willing to face them means you are already winning. Trust me, you will fall short on some of the things you try to do—but this is not failure. Failure comes only when you give up. These will be learning experiences that you can build a foundation on for your future and future successes.

Go for it. Think of something that you have always wanted in your life but you did not get because you were afraid. It could be an activity, job, travel, or a relationship. Be willing to take a chance and face the fear. You will find peace on the other side.

## *The Gift of Purpose*

How many people do you know who are going through life just existing rather than living a fulfilled life? I know of many. They are living a routine with no goals or purpose. We all have things that we have to do in life. Work is usually the main activity done without a reason other than to "put food on the table and a roof over our head." But to make a living without a purpose is nothing more than killing time. I have worked those types of jobs, and at the end of the day have felt empty.

One of the greatest forms of punishment for any person would be to take away their sense of purpose in life. To spend a life without a reason for doing what you do is pointless and makes you feel empty. What are you working for? What is the purpose of what you are doing? Is it just to make money? That can be the shallowest reason to work. What if it is to make money to give to a just cause? Now there's a purpose. What if you worked to make money to help the misfortunate in your city? Again, now you have a reason for working and living.

If you feel lost with no sense of direction, you need to find a purpose for your life. You need to look *inside* yourself and find out what would make you feel complete. Then you need to look *outside* yourself, look at your neighbors, coworkers, community, church, country, and see what needs you can help meet.

As I have stated before, you are a creative being. If you work all day long with no purpose other than survival, you will lose your zeal for life. Find your purpose and reason for living; otherwise you will be destined to the same fate as those who die and leave nothing to this world other than a dash between the birth and death dates on their tombstone.

A great way to get started is to ask yourself what it is that you would like to do that would make you feel complete. What is that thing that defines you as a person? If you could do anything you wanted and you knew you would be a success what would that one thing be? Start with that question. I bet once you answer that, you could do that thing and have a positive impact on the people around you.

Find your purpose and live for it.

## *The Gift of Choice*

Choice is the fundamental building block of our lives. The life you are living right now was created by the choices you have made to this point. Your future will be determined by the choices you make from this point forward. You make choices every day whether you know it or not. Those choices are creating your life each waking moment.

I believe the greatest gift that God gave humankind is the ability to choose. It allows you to create your life to be what you want it to be. This is true for those who understand it and for those who don't. You can become a slave to the choices you make without any thought to their importance. Those who don't understand the power of choice make choices—by *not* making choices. They let things around them happen and then are led around by others who are making choices. Every day leads to your future; and every day you are not making choices leading you to where you want to go, is a choice taking you away from your desired future.

When you understand the power of choice you can use it to create a path to life, not death. Every goal requires a journey and every journey requires steps. If you want to take a trip from New York to Los Angeles, you can't just step out your door and be there. First you have to choose the dates of your trip, then you have to choose between the different modes of transportation. Next you will buy the transportation ticket, and then choose what clothes to pack. You will probably need to choose a rental car when you arrive, and you will have to choose what motel to reserve for your stay.

Your life is just like a trip. You need to choose where you want to go, when you want to get there, what you need to take along and leave behind. Unless you plan your life's journey, you will never get beyond where you are now. Those who have what they want and are where they want to be, got there by hard work, planning, and making the right choices. They realize that every choice they make affects their future.

Some people say, "One day I will do this or that," but they make no plans to do it. They think that someone will come along and give them an opportunity or hand them their dream. The fact is, unless you set your destination and make a step-by-step plan to get there, you will be sitting at the same place this time next year. If you want to do something in life, you need to identify it, speak it, write it down, and make a plan. Then work the plan. You will have to make adjustments along the way, but that is OK.

You have the ability to choose the course of your journey and plan your final destination.

Remember that all along the way, the choices you make every day lead you to your final outcome—the life you have built on all the gifts in your life.

## The Gift of Forgiveness

Much like fear, unforgiveness is a prison. It holds you in chains of self-pity. It keeps your focus on yourself and causes you to have a warped sense of reality. You see everything through self-colored glasses. Until you let go of the unforgiveness in your life, you will be held back from any mental or spiritual growth. You will not be able to move on in certain areas of your life because there will always be something to remind you of the unforgiveness in your life.

Unforgiveness can be very deceiving. You may think that holding on to unforgiveness in some way punishes the person that you have not forgiven. In reality, that person has moved on and most likely doesn't even know that you have an issue with them. The only person being punished is you. Because you are the one holding on to the unforgiveness, you are the only one affected by it.

You must be careful because this way of life can become normal to you. You create a false sense of comfort; so when you have the opportunity to forgive, you decide not to because you have created a false reality. You become trapped in a lifestyle of unforgiveness. In some strange way, you can even feel justified by not forgiving that person. This form of self-righteousness can be a trap as well.

The good news—there is a way out. It comes back to retraining your mind. Start filling your mind with thoughts and words of forgiveness. Identify the person and issue that you are dealing with and decide to forgive. Get a piece of paper and write something like: *I forgive _____ for what he/she has done to me. I let go of all feelings of anger and bitterness.* Then put it somewhere where you will see it every day. When you see it, you need to say it out loud. Do this several times each day for a week. You may feel funny doing this, but you will be feeding your subconscious in this area, and you will be training your mind. When you do that, your thoughts will gravitate toward forgiveness and you will become a person of forgiveness instead of unforgiveness.

Unforgiveness will stop you from being the person you need to be. Don't let it be part of your life. True peace is found in the heart of a forgiving person. Choose life and create the life you want to have.

You can do whatever you want in life, and you can be whoever you want to be. Make the right choices. Accept the gifts that your Creator has given you.

# More About Tracy J. Trost

*T*rost Moving Pictures is an independent film production company based in Tulsa, OK and has been making waves in the entertainment arena. Their first multi-award winning film *Find Me*, has been awarded both Best Feature and Best Actor at multiple film festivals. Their second film, *A Christmas Snow*, is set to be released nationwide in 2010 through Destiny Image Films and stars: Catherine Mary Stewart (*The Last Starfighter*), Muse Watson (*Prison Break, NCIS*), Anthony Tyler Quinn (*No Greater Love, Boy Meets World*), and Cameron ten Napel (*Super, Pink*).

They are actively pursuing many exciting projects in the entertainment industry, including their next feature film, *The Lamp*, with best-selling author Jim Stovall, Author of the best-selling book *The Ultimate Gift*, which the film, *The Ultimate Gift* by 20th Century Fox and Fox Faith was based on.

You can find out more about them at any of their sites:

TrostMovingPictures.com

aChristmasSnow.com

FindMeTheMovie.com

Twitter.com/TMPics

Facebook.com/TMPics

Facebook.com/aChristmasSnow

Dear Reader,

I want to thank your for taking a walk with Sam and his journey of discovery.

As he discovered in the last days of his life carrying the hurts and pains of the past do only one thing.

They hold you back from who you can be, and I believe who you should be. In the following pages you will find four chapters from

The Novel A Christmas Snow that my good friend Jim Stovall so graciously wrote based on the movie A Christmas Snow.

If you have not read this book or seen the movie A Christmas Snow then I encourage you to do so.

A Christmas Snow tells the story of Kathleen Mitchell and her path to finding freedom and healing in forgiveness.

If you have enjoyed this book I encourage you to purchase more copies and give them to your friends and family.

Books such as Restored and A Christmas Snow have a way of reaching people in a way that no person can and help them to become more of who they should be in their lives.

Once again I thank you for taking the time to read this book.

I hope it has touched you in a way that will have eternal impact on your life.

Tracy J Trost

*Chapter One*

he snowfall that blanketed the town that particular year became legendary and was special for several reasons. First, the snow that year was light and fluffy. It fell in huge, artistic flakes that painted the entire cityscape and countryside like a carpet of diamonds. It was nothing like the annoying wintry mix that people in the town suffer through each winter, made up predominantly of black ice and gray sleet pellets, covered by mountains of drifting frozen snow.

The snow that particular year was special for one other very important reason. It fell at Christmastime.

A white Christmas is not just something that people in Minnesota sing about or watch in movies. It is an ordeal they annually struggle through. It makes decorating and holiday shopping a chore while inflicting hardships on friends and family trying to visit the area or residents attempting to travel out of town for holiday celebrations elsewhere.

The snow that fell that year was not accompanied by sleet or ice. It arrived just before Christmas, was easy to get around in, and wondrous to look at. That magical snow signaled to everyone that it was going to be a special Christmas that year.

The traditional Christmas songs sung by strolling carolers seemed to have a little more hope and energy than previous years. The Christmas lights were brighter, and each decoration seemed new and pristine like the wonderful snow.

This was especially true at the Mitchell residence, a white, ranch-style home where 10-year-old Kathleen was convinced that the holiday this year was certainly better than anything contained in her previous Christmas memories. She was decked out in her snowflake pajamas and lying on the floor, gazing up at the glorious Christmas tree that was arranged in front of the picture window in the Mitchell living room.

Like the snow, the tree this year was simply better than ever before. It boasted strings of popcorn she had created herself, along with an assortment of garlands, some new store-bought ornaments, and some of her family's traditional hand-crafted decorations. A star glistened from the treetop, and everything seemed to be in its place.

It was all special to her, but Kathleen's absolute favorite was the solitary white porcelain angel ornament she had prominently displayed on the exact, perfect branch of the Christmas tree.

Kathleen was lost in her thoughts of holidays past and what promise the bright and shiny packages under the tree might hold for her.

Her reverie was broken by the angry voices of her parents' current argument that drifted to her through the open doorway of their bedroom. Their hostility and vicious words blended with the background Christmas music, creating a macabre symphony and an ominous ballet. Although Kathleen tried to ignore it, these verbal battles between her parents had become more frequent and more vicious in recent days.

Kathleen sighed deeply and tried to refocus her attention on the beautiful Christmas tree. She crawled under the branches to try to gain a new perspective and escape from the increasingly intrusive sound of her parents' argument invading the living room. Kathleen shut her eyes and tried to focus on the magical Christmas celebration that she had been looking forward to ever since she had finished her last piece of Thanksgiving pumpkin pie.

Her holiday thoughts were interrupted by the sound of her father's approaching solid footsteps. She rolled over and opened her eyes in time to see his strides, punctuated by a swinging suitcase, as he passed the Christmas tree, opened the front door, and solidly slammed it behind him with finality.

Kathleen had seen her father leave the house many times and for many reasons, but deep down in her soul, she knew something was different today.

She leapt to her feet and gazed out the picture window as her father crossed the snow-covered yard. Kathleen knocked on the window, and her father stopped and turned so he could look over his shoulder and see her framed in the window with the backdrop of the Christmas tree behind her. Then, without expression, he deliberately turned and simply walked away.

As Kathleen watched her father's back retreating into the snow and dark night, a single tear rolled down her cheek and fell.

*Chapter Two*

Although three tumultuous decades had come and gone, Kathleen still remembered that long-ago glistening tear as a drop of water fell into her bathroom sink. She gazed into the bathroom mirror before her, looking upon what other people thought was her stunning face; but as usual, her expression was firmly closed off, and she simply didn't give much away.

The 40-year-old image that gazed back at her did not please her, not because she didn't like it, but because that kind of thought or emotion would have to reach Kathleen at a place she had closed and locked 30 years before.

Just then, a timer buzzed, and Kathleen removed a teeth whitening strip, rinsed with water, inspected her already impeccably white teeth, and grimaced. She opened her color-coordinated medicine cabinet and loaded her toothbrush for one more cleaning.

Kathleen's entire life was made up of a series of daily routines and rituals.

A few minutes later, as was her custom, Kathleen dressed in her color-coordinated jogging suit that was the latest fashion in sports-wear, with her iPod strapped to her arm and her ear buds in place.

Over the years, and especially each winter, she was glad she had left Minnesota far behind, along with its Arctic weather and painful mem-ories. Here in Tulsa, Oklahoma, you could run outdoors virtually year 'round.

Kathleen managed to jog her regular route through the neighborhood and around a nearby park without noticing any of her neighbors waving at her or the wonderful scenery around her. She just put one foot in front of the other until she was back in front of her house.

She slowly walked across her yard as her breathing calmed and her heart rate approached normal. As she moved along her front walkway and approached the front porch, she saw the morning newspaper perched on the front steps.

Kathleen turned off her iPod, took out her ear buds, and reached down for the morning newspaper. As she held it in her hand, she saw her own picture staring back at her from the corner of the front page of one of the sections of the paper. She looked at her own image that she had known would be there. She looked away and walked into her house.

Kathleen marched into her kitchen and threw the paper onto the counter. It landed with her picture staring at her once again from the top corner. She began loading an assortment of fruits, juices, and various powders into her blender. She hit the button, and the blender whirred into action. Only then did Kathleen allow her attention to move back to the newspaper lying on the counter.

She concluded her normal morning routine in the kitchen with the paper closed and her picture staring at her the whole time. As usual, she was in control of her emotions, and whatever was in the newspaper about her would simply not be allowed to affect her resolve.

Only when Kathleen was completely ready for work according to her usual high standards did she walk into the kitchen, finally opening the newspaper to reveal what was inside. She removed Sections A and B, which she immediately tossed into the recycling bin, leaving Section C, the Food and Wine Section, laying open before her.

On the cover of the Food and Wine Section of the morning newspaper, there was a picture of Kathleen with an uncomfortable expression on her face. She was holding a turkey. The bold headline read, NOT QUITE HOME FOR THE HOLIDAYS. Kathleen immediately refolded the section of the newspaper and tossed it into the recycling bin to join the other discarded sections.

Even though she had decided she wouldn't give them the satisfaction of reading the article or letting it affect her in any way, a short time later she found herself furiously scrubbing a drinking glass full of soapy water in the sink as she stared at the now-soiled front page of the Food and Wine Section on the counter beside her.

Kathleen was so distracted by the newspaper that she absentmindedly picked up the glass of soapy water and took a big drink from it. She gagged and let out a frustrated cry as she stormed into the bathroom to brush her teeth once again.

As Kathleen went into her autopilot mode and rapidly backed her car out of her garage and into the street, she failed to notice a delivery truck stopping in front of her house. The driver hopped out and rushed onto the porch. After ringing the doorbell repeatedly, he left a small brown package beside Kathleen's front door.

As Kathleen drove to work that day, she spread open that same Food and Wine Section of the morning newspaper across her steering wheel. At a red light, she read the vicious words and exclaimed aloud to herself, "Comfort food has never been so cold."

Just then her cell phone rang, and she picked it up. She answered automatically without checking the caller ID, knowing that it had to be someone from work calling about the newspaper article. Without saying hello or uttering a greeting of any kind, she stated, "I'm reading it right now. And, no, it doesn't mean we're closing for Christmas."

Kathleen heard an uncomfortable silence on her cell phone followed by the bewildered and unexpected voice of her mother repeating, "Hello. Hello?"

Kathleen refused to let the usual flood of emotions created by her mother's voice wash over her. She simply closed the phone and tossed it onto the seat beside her. She was so distracted that she did not notice the light had changed or anything else until the phone on the seat beside her insistently rang again.

The caller ID confirmed to Kathleen that her mother was persistent that morning. She ignored the ringing phone and accelerated through the intersection. She couldn't deal with the multitude of emotions and feelings, so, as usual, she simply blocked them out and drove to work.

# Chapter Three

Tulsa, Oklahoma, is a unique community. Depending upon whom you speak with, Tulsa is either a large town or a small city. It has many of the amenities and features of a world class metropolis, but people tend to know each other or at least know people who know people, like a small town.

Kathleen drove without thinking along her standard route into downtown Tulsa and parked her car in her usual parking space. As she walked down the sidewalk, she spotted the sign on the awning outside her business that proclaimed

*Kathleen's Ti Amo's Restaurant.* It was a classic Italian eatery housed in a beautiful 1940s era brick building. Most people would feel a sense of pride or accomplishment as they walked beneath such an awning on their way to work each day. The most Kathleen could muster was a mild sense of satisfaction as she walked through the front door of her restaurant that morning.

As she entered, the early morning crew was busily cleaning up and getting everything in readiness for the luncheon crowd. The second that everyone became aware of Kathleen's presence, the fun and camaraderie among the employees disappeared. Kathleen's presence was like a wet blanket that dampened the spirits of all who made their living at *Kathleen's Ti Amo's Restaurant.*

If Kathleen was aware of this, she gave off no sign of recognition. She simply acknowledged everyone present with a monotone, "Morning."

Her greeting was met with absolute silence until Martin, a heavyset man of 50, mustered the courage to respond. "Good morning, my dear."

Kathleen cut to the chase: "I know you've read it, so you can stop with all the pleasantries."

Martin, feigning innocence, asked, "Read what, my dear?"

"The article in all of the newspapers I'm sure you hid when I walked in." Kathleen held out her hands and demanded, "C'mon, hand them over."

A guilty-looking busboy pulled a paper from beneath a table cloth.

Martin looked at the newspaper Kathleen now held in her tightly clenched fist and said, "Oh, yes. *That* newspaper."

Kathleen nodded emphatically. "Yes, *this* newspaper."

Martin presented a peace offering, saying, "It's really not so bad."

"They called me a Gourmet Grinch. I've never read so many bad puns in my life." Kathleen glared.

"It's just the small town mentality. Everyone should be with their families on Christmas."

"We're like a family. Right?" Kathleen inquired of everyone. The staff fell completely silent.

Chef Claud, a round man of 42, popped his head in from the kitchen. Kathleen looked at Claud for the answer to her question. "Right?"

Claud shrugged and said, "I guess. Like a dysfunctional family."

"Who never goes on vacation," Martin chimed in.

"Funny," Kathleen shot back sarcastically.

Martin smiled. "Almost as funny as this." He handed her a note.

Kathleen sighed in frustration. "Ugh. My mother is relentless."

Martin pursed his lips. "Shouldn't you just talk to her? She said it was urgent."

Kathleen waved it off. "It's just her annual Christmas invitation."

"It really wouldn't hurt to close the restaurant for a day," Claud inserted.

Kathleen shook her head definitively. "Not a chance. I have mouths to feed."

Martin and Claud exchanged knowing glances and, finally, Claud mumbled, "Not after that article."

"I won't abandon all of our loyal holiday loners," Kathleen said emphatically. "Besides, how..."

Martin and Claud completed her sentence in unison. "How can we feed them if we aren't open?" They both laughed.

Martin looked at Kathleen. "Then we'd better rethink your Christmas gift."

"Oh, yeah?" Kathleen shot back.

Martin responded, "We were all gonna pitch in to change the locks."

Kathleen appeared frustrated as she crumpled up the phone message from her mother.

Martin and Claud laughed again, and Claud sighed in relief and said to Martin, "Whew! I could kiss you."

Martin got a mischievous look on his face and said, conspiratorially, "Speaking of which…" as he walked to his maitre d' stand and pulled out a branch of mistletoe. He snuck up behind Kathleen who was busy looking over the day's reservations. As he moved in close, Kathleen demanded, "Stop."

Martin began making kissing sounds.

Kathleen turned around and said, "Stop that. What in the…" She sighed and continued, "If you don't put that away, I'm gonna…"

Claud interrupted saying, "What? Have some fun? You're a prude."

Kathleen shot back, "Yes, I'm a prude. A Christmas prude. Now get back to work."

As Kathleen walked toward her office, Martin whispered to Claud, "She's the prude who stole Christmas."

Kathleen said, "I heard that," as she continued walking to her office.

Martin cleared his throat and addressed all of the employees in the dining room, announcing, "Half hour until doors open."

*Chapter Four*

**D**owntown Tulsa boasts a smorgasbord of architecture. There are the same type of new steel and glass monstrosities evident in any major metropolitan area, and then there are some marvelous art deco buildings that are holdovers from the oil boom and the wealth that flowed in the first half of the last century.

At midday, workers rush out of these buildings to try to get a brief bite of lunch during their limited lunch hour or to have a more leisurely meal while discussing business with prospects or colleagues.

Kathleen had always taken a great deal of satisfaction from the fact that her restaurant had a great reputation with the lunch crowd. People could either get in and out quickly while still having some quality food or linger over a multi-course meal while doing business.

The dining room was full once again, and Martin was deftly making his way from table to table, greeting diners and making sure everything was up to Kathleen's high standards.

Kathleen had retreated to her office where she was trying to deal with the myriad of emotions that were competing inside of her head. Without thinking, she unwrapped a chocolate Santa Claus. She took a calculating look at the chocolate holiday figure before she viciously and thoroughly bit Santa's head off and began chewing.

Martin stuck his head through her office doorway. Kathleen greeted him with "Go away, I'm hiding."

Martin persisted, "I think you might want to see this."

Kathleen moved over to the open door where Martin stood, and followed his gaze toward a table across the dining room where the food critic who had written the awful newspaper review was casually seated.

"What's he doing here?" Without waiting for an answer, Kathleen charged toward the table, blurting out, "You've got a lot of nerve coming to my restaurant after that review."

The food critic looked up at her calmly and said, "Why, Kathleen. Your food is great. There's just no Christmas cheer in here."

Kathleen was about to let him have it, but Martin interceded to save the other luncheon diners from hearing her forthcoming verbal onslaught. "Um, Kathleen. You have a call holding."

Kathleen glared at the food critic and tried to dismiss Martin. "Tell her I'm busy with a customer."

"It's not your mother."

Kathleen's attention was diverted away from the vengeance she was planning to inflict on the food critic as she turned curiously toward Martin.

"It's a handsome gentleman caller," Martin explained.

Kathleen's countenance and entire attitude immediately changed. "Andrew! I could use some good news today."

Giving the food critic one more threatening glare, Kathleen turned and strode toward the bar, where she picked up the phone and said without any greeting, "Please don't tell me you're calling to cancel."

Across town, Andrew—a handsome businessman—was sitting at his desk in his office as he responded, "Not canceling...but there's a little change of plans."

Kathleen gripped the phone tightly and said, "So, you've read the article."

A loud chuckle was all the response she got from Andrew before he said, "No. In fact I'm bringing you more business."

Kathleen inquired curiously, "Oh, yeah? How much more?"

He responded, "Just one other person—my daughter."

Kathleen grimaced and tried to keep some of the frustration and trepidation out of her voice, "Oh. That's great."

The magical dinner she had been planning in her restaurant that night with Andrew, and the special evening she was anticipating after dinner, disappeared into thin air like a mirage in the desert.